MAXIMUM
SELF-ESTEEM

MAXIMUM
SELF-ESTEEM

—

The Handbook For Reclaiming
Your Sense of Self-Worth

Jerry Minchinton

ARNFORD HOUSE, PUBLISHERS
a division of the arnford corporation

Copyright Acknowledgments appear on page 253

Publisher's Cataloging in Publication

Minchinton, Jerry A.
   Maximum self-esteem : the handbook for reclaiming your sense of self-worth / Jerry Arnold Minchinton.
   p. cm.
   Includes bibliographical references.
   Preassigned LCCN: 92-076034.
   ISBN 0-9635719-7-4

   1. Self-esteem. I. Title.

BF697.5.S46M55 1993   158'.1
         QBI93-454

Printed in the United States of America

20 19 18 17

CONTENTS

Acknowledgments

This book has been greatly improved by the help of a number of busy people who, despite having their hands full with projects of their own, generously consented to give me their criticisms and suggestions. I am indebted to long-time friend and associate, Clif Bradley, who followed my project closely from the beginning and patiently read more drafts of this book than anyone should have had to. I am grateful to Jean Names and Stacy Gilbert, two wonderful individuals for whom the word *supportive* could have been coined, who gave me the benefit of their caring insight, creative wisdom, advice, and sense of humor. My thanks to John Moore, whose observations persuaded me to revise my opinion on certain key points. I am also indebted to Suzanne Sutherland, of Mountain Home Technical College in Arkansas, not just for her valuable editorial assistance, but for her contagious enthusiasm as well.

Preface

I became interested in self-esteem several years ago when my business partner and I decided to use it as the basis for a pre-employment test. We had observed a connection between our employees' self-esteem and their work habits, so we concluded that by using a test to measure job candidates' self-esteem, we could better match employees to jobs.

When I began my research, I found self-esteem was largely unexplored territory. Although its significance seems obvious, there was little information available about this important subject. Most mental health professionals were acquainted with the idea of self-esteem, but with few exceptions, they didn't know where it came from, agree on what it was, or have even a vague idea of how to improve it.

Fortunately, the body of literature on self-esteem has grown over the past several years. This is due in a large part to the interest and publicity generated by California's *Task Force to Promote Self-Esteem and Personal and Social Responsibility*. (Almost as if to underscore that the study of self-esteem was in its infancy, the task force took months just to define the term.) Despite this increase, there is still a shortage of practical information on how self-esteem can be improved. While many books tell us we *should* feel good about ourselves, they fail to provide concrete and believable reasons *why* and clear explanations as to *how*. This book is written with the intention of bridging this gap.

In the course of studying how to gauge others' self-esteem, I made two discoveries. First, my own self-esteem had improved remarkably. Evidently, as I read about the principles of high self-esteem, I had absorbed them to a certain extent. But most important, I realized that *in all cases poor self-regard was due to certain incorrect core beliefs.* This being true, I reasoned the most direct route to improving self-esteem was to become aware of and accept *accurate* beliefs in place of the inaccurate ones.

If this sounds too easy, it is because we have too little faith in simple, uninvolved solutions to psychological problems. We prefer them to be lengthy and complicated. But after all, what *is* poor self-esteem but believing we are inherently unworthy? And if low self-esteem is a matter of belief, then high self-esteem must be, too.

The idea that incorrect beliefs have a negative impact on us is not a new one. As Dr. Albert Ellis pointed out over thirty years ago, irrational beliefs and ideas often prevent us from functioning in a psychologically healthy manner. In *Reason and Emotion in Psychotherapy*, he states:

> In existing societies our family and other institutions directly and indirectly indoctrinate all of us so that we grow up to believe many superstitious, senseless ideas. ... many of our most cherished and dogmatically upheld values...are only *assumed* to be "good" values and are rarely seriously reviewed or questioned by those who keep drumming them into the heads of our children.

Maximum Self-Esteem brings to light our irrational beliefs about ourselves, our relationships, and life in general. These false assumptions, because they cause us to dislike ourselves, have a devastating, crippling effect on us and every aspect of our lives. This book explores those beliefs, traces their origin, explains how believing them makes us think poorly of ourselves, and then presents accurate, self-esteem-enhancing beliefs to replace those which cause so much harm.

But is self-esteem truly so important? Is it worth all the fuss currently being made over it? Anyone who doubts its relevance need only read a daily newspaper. There he or she will discover an increasing incidence of vandalism, fraud, theft, robbery, rape, child abuse, battered spouses, murder, hate crimes, genocide (now termed "ethnic cleansing"), along with a multitude of other senseless, violent acts that have become disturbingly common. *These are not the actions of people who like themselves.*

There is no doubt in my mind that the solution to a great many problems, whether personal, national, or global, lies in improving our feelings about ourselves both as individuals and as members of society. When the significance of good self-esteem is better understood and it achieves the prominence it deserves, a transformation will begin. As the people on this planet learn they are deserving of self-respect, their respect for others will automatically increase.

* * *

Introduction

How do you know the ideas in this book will work? You don't, of course, and the only way to find out if they do is by trying them. As a matter of principle, *don't accept **anything**, including what you read in this book, as true without first subjecting it to reasonable verification.* It is beneficial to maintain a healthy skepticism. The majority of our problems have occurred because we accepted misinformation as true, and went on to behave as though it were. Refusing to accept others' "facts" as true until we have personally verified them is a sign of personal growth, rather than stubbornness.

Consider the ideas presented here only as working hypotheses. Give them your serious consideration. Examine them logically. Think about them. Test them. Try them out. Then, *based on your own experience,* decide whether they are true. It is not necessary to *believe* the ideas in this book to make them start working for you; just consider the possibility that they may be true, and then suspend your disbelief long enough to give them a try.

A Matter of Definition

1) The words "parent" or "parents," as used in this book, refer to the caregivers and authority figures who played a significant part in our early upbringing and were responsible for shaping our ideas of ourselves and the world. This might be our biological parents, but it could also be brothers, sisters, other relatives, adoptive or foster parents, teachers, or anyone else who had a strong influence on us.

2) When the word *problem* is used, unless a problem of a physical nature is specified, it should be understood to be either *emotional* or *psychological.*

3) I use first person plural fairly consistently throughout this book. So, rather than seeing "I," "me," or "my," you will usually find "we," "us," and "our." This is because the problems discussed here are universal problems shared by us all.

Using This Book

For obvious reasons, *you* are the only person who can make a permanent and positive change in your self-esteem. Making this change will require a certain amount of commitment on your part.

It will take time and effort. There are no quick fixes here, just solid, substantial truths about you and your life. If they are to work for you, these ideas must be understood and absorbed. To be honest about it, you will have to *live* with the ideas in this book. They are intended to eliminate the causes of low self-esteem, rather than just the symptoms, so they must be experienced, as well as read.

It is necessary to put the principles into practice. Intellectual understanding alone is of little help. You will notice improvement in your self-esteem when you begin applying these principles. How long it takes for this to happen is up to you. Since the results depend largely on your own efforts, no one can hold you back; you can set your own pace and work as rapidly as you choose. Only *you* will know when you have reached the level of self-esteem where you feel comfortable.

Be totally honest with yourself. You are bound to encounter what appear to be unpleasant facts about yourself. Disagreeable though they may be, only by facing them can you begin to change them. Ignoring facts that are inconvenient or uncomfortable will not make them less true. Unless you are willing to admit there is something wrong in your life, you will not try to fix it. When you *do* encounter unpalatable facts about yourself, don't beat yourself up with them, simply accept that they exist.

Be open to new ideas and concepts. You may feel that turning your back on some of your old (if painful) beliefs is like denying old friends. It may seem to you, as it did to me, that by giving up long-held opinions and beliefs I was giving up important parts of myself and would no longer be the same person. In a sense, this is true, but it is just the opposite of unpleasant.

Once your incorrect, painful beliefs are gone, you will not feel a sense of loss, but of great relief. If you want to improve your life, be receptive to ideas that will help you do so. Don't assume you already know the truth; it is hard to do this and keep an open mind.

Don't confuse *intellectual* knowing with *practical* knowing. As you read some of the ideas in this book, you may say, "Why, I already know that." That may be true, but bear in mind that mental acceptance is not necessarily the same as actual belief. Many times we accept ideas on an intellectual level because they are logical, but fail to apply them to real-life situations. While intellectual acceptance is an important first step, unless our day-to-day actions prove we believe something to be true, it may as well not be. If you come across a Mistaken Belief you already consider wrong you may be inclined to disregard the chapter that focuses on it. But before you decide to skip it, ask yourself if your actions prove — *beyond a doubt* — that you believe it. If they do, then move on to another belief you think is true.

Be willing to change. We are reluctant to change, even when we know doing so will improve the quality of our lives. We tend to think of ourselves as though we were born fully-formed, so to speak, with our likes, dislikes, habits, opinions, speech and thought patterns, and so forth, already in place.

Actually, our personality develops a little at a time and continues to grow and change throughout our entire life. So, like it or not, we are subject to continual change. Since change is inevitable, we may as well select modifications that improve our lives. If we have a sincere desire to increase our self-esteem, we must expect change because without it, progress is impossible.

You need to be aware you will sometimes be unsuccessful. We are inclined to forget most successes are preceded by a number of *non*-successes. That is why it makes sense to regard situations that turn out differently than we want as *feedback*, rather than failures. We do not fail — we simply find out what does and does not work. This is not clever talk to make you feel good; it is the way life actually is. Think of yourself as a guided missile, aimed at success; although your goal may elude you temporarily, attaining it is just a matter of adjusting your course little by little till you finally hit your target.

You will find an improvement in one area of your self-esteem has a sort of "ripple effect" on other areas. No matter where we start making changes, each success makes future successes easier. When we first begin improving our self-esteem, the changes may be barely perceptible. As we continue, changes occur on deeper levels of the mind and then radiate out to affect every aspect of ourselves.

How *Maximum Self-Esteem* is Arranged

The body of this book is divided into two parts. **Part I** contains a self-esteem inventory, to give you an idea of your feelings about yourself. This is followed by information about self-esteem: what it is and is not; why we are lacking in self-esteem; what we can do to improve our feelings about ourselves, and techniques to help with this process.

Most chapters in **Part II** are centered on exploring specific ideas responsible for low self-esteem. Each of these inaccurate beliefs is labeled a "Mistaken Belief." Later in the same chapter a "Counter-Belief" will be identified. With the exception of the Chapters "Manipulation" and "Verbal Traps," **Part II** may be read in any order the reader chooses.

If you read *Maximum Self-Esteem* from cover to cover, you will notice certain key points appear in more than one chapter. This is intentional. Since the chapters in **Part II** need not be read sequentially, it is important that each chapter be complete in itself, rather than depending on earlier chapters to provide a foundation for it. To be sure they were not overlooked, I have repeated certain fundamental ideas in closely-related chapters.

A note of caution: Before putting the principles contained in this book into use, I advise you to carefully consider how they may affect your life situation. Even the most beneficial of tools can be harmful if used inappropriately or without consideration of the consequences.

Making This Book Work For You

I suggest you read *Maximum Self-Esteem* from beginning to end to familiarize yourself with the basic concepts and get an overview of the subject. Then begin again at **Part II** and read all or part of a chapter each day, preferably just after you wake up. Repeated reading of these essays is important because it makes their ideas familiar and comfortable. You may choose a different chapter each day or repeat the same one until it is thoroughly familiar. The biggest help, you will find, is continued exposure to the facts contained in this book.

Make what you read a part of your day. Write down, or highlight the most important points so you can refresh your memory throughout the day. Think about the ideas often; look for situations that illustrate how they affect your life and the lives of others.

There are exercises at the end of most chapters. Use them. They are developed to help you attain a working knowledge of principles and ideas that will increase your self-esteem. Since many involve writing, you may find it helpful to use a notebook or a binder.

Now, with the preliminary material out of the way, here is my invitation: read this book and put its principles into practice. If you do, I promise your life will undergo a dramatic change for the better. The world will seem a much nicer place to live, and you will feel more relaxed, comfortable, and happier than you have in years. Remember — of all the judgements we make in our life, the judgement we make about ourselves is the most important by far.

* * *

PART I

SELF-ESTEEM

1

Self-Esteem Inventory

This is an inventory, not a test; there are no right or wrong answers. It is a tool with which to gauge your progress as you work with this book. Once you have taken it, you can re-take it at intervals to measure your growth and see which areas need further improvement. There is a similar Inventory in the appendix at the end of this volume. Alternate between the two inventories to track your improvement. The statements in the inventory are typically true of persons with good self-esteem. Your goal is to make them true of you.

Write the numbers 1 through 25 down the left hand side of a page in your notebook. Then, read through the self-esteem inventory and put a number rating next to each number on the sheet. Rate your responses as to how true each of the statements are of you.

1 = I NEVER do
2 = I OCCASIONALLY do
3 = I USUALLY do
4 = I ALWAYS do

1) I accept myself fully just as I am.
2) I believe others behave as they do for good reasons.
3) My opinion of myself is more important than others' opinions of me.
4) If I recall the past, I concentrate on only pleasant memories
5) I forgive myself for my mistakes.
6) I do not punish myself for my mistakes by feeling guilty.
7) I like myself regardless of how others feel.
8) I am not afraid of failure or defeat.
9) I do not compare myself unfavorably with others.
10) I feel worthwhile even when I do things imperfectly.
11) I am as important as anyone else.
12) I do not allow anyone to persuade me to do things against my better judgement.
13) I allow others to experience the consequences of their actions.
14) When I want people to do something for me, I ask them directly.
15) I regard problems as opportunities to improve my life
16) I am flexible enough to adjust to any circumstances I face.
17) I see each incident in life as beneficial to me in some way.
18) I do not insist others adopt my standards and ideals.
19) I accept full responsibility for my problems.
20) I control all my behavior, including my habits.
21. I do not punish myself by feeling bad.
22) I do not accept the blame for others' painful feelings.
23) I do not look up to or down on anyone.
24) I accept nothing as true without reasonable verification.
25) I encourage others to grow and mature rather than to depend on me.

Now add all the numbers to arrive at your score. The result will be a percentile indicating which areas need some work. Don't be concerned if you've found there's room for improvement. Your place on the self-esteem scale at present is unimportant. We are not by any means finished products. As human beings, we have unlimited potential for positive change. If you have desire and determination and are willing to invest some time and energy in enhancing your self-regard, you will be where you want to be.

Those statements you've marked with the lowest numbers are the areas in which there is most room for improvement. If you choose to begin working on those, rather than reading from beginning to end, the numbers of the statements are followed by the number of the chapter to which they relate. No matter which method you decide on, it is important you read the next three chapters because they establish the foundation for the information in **Part II**.

1 - Chapter 5	14 - Chapters 14, 15
2 - Chapter 6	15 - Chapter 19
3 - Chapter 11	16 - Chapter 17
4 - Chapter 8	17 - Chapter 18
5 - Chapter 9	18 - Chapter 6
6 - Chapter 10	19 - Chapter 19
7 - Chapter 11	20 - Chapter 16
8 - Chapter 12	21 - Chapter 7
9 - Chapter 5	22 - Chapter 7
10 - Chapter 13	23 - Chapter 20
11 - Chapter 5	24 - Chapter 21
12 - Chapters 14, 15	25 - Chapter 22
13 - Chapter 22	

* * *

2

What is Self-Esteem?

THE NATURE OF SELF-ESTEEM

Self-esteem is the value we place on ourselves. It is our assessment of our worth as a human being, based on our approval or disapproval of ourselves and our behavior. We could also describe it as the regard in which we hold ourselves, or our feelings about ourselves based on who and what we believe we are. It is more, though, than just whether we think we are an OK person. Self-esteem isn't a single quality or aspect; in its broader sense, it is a combination of related traits and attitudes. In terms of its importance, self-esteem is our center — the basis upon which we build our lives. And since we do not live in isolation from the rest of the world, the way we feel about ourselves affects how we relate to the people around us and to every other aspect of life.

THE THREE ASPECTS OF SELF-ESTEEM

While everyone *has* self-esteem, only a small percentage of us have *high* self-esteem. What are the differences between good and poor self-esteem, between having a positive or a negative opinion of ourselves? Here are the three aspects of self-esteem, examined from the perspectives of both high and low self-esteem.

ASPECT ONE: OUR FEELINGS ABOUT OURSELVES

With HIGH self-esteem, *we accept ourselves unconditionally exactly as we are; we appreciate our value as a human being.*

- "Unquestioning and unconditional" mean our acceptance and appreciation of ourselves are independent of *anything* about us, other than that we exist. Simply put, we accept ourselves fully; we feel comfortable with, and good about ourselves, *no matter what.* We value our uniqueness as individuals, regardless of any traits, abilities, or skills we do or do not possess.
- We have self-respect and a deep-seated belief that we are important and we matter, if not to others, at least to ourselves. High self-esteem means we are compassionate and forgiving toward ourselves; we like ourselves, imperfections and all.
- We appreciate our personal worth, so we are unaffected by others' opinions; we do not feel better when we are praised or worse when we are criticized. Our good feelings about ourselves do not rely on any exterior conditions or on anything we may do or have done.
- We are in control of our emotions. To a large extent, we are free from the unpleasant feelings of guilt, anger, fear, and sadness. Our strongest and most common emotion is happiness, which occurs

simply because we are pleased with ourselves and our lives.

When we have LOW self-esteem, *we believe we have little intrinsic worth. We believe our personal value is in direct proportion to the value of our accomplishments.*

• Some of us try too hard and become highly competitive workaholics and over-achievers. With few genuine feelings of self-worth, we try to create some and prove we are somebody by our successes and achievements. Because our desire for perfection is so great, we set unrealistic goals and place unreasonable demands on ourselves. Failing, rather than encouraging us to have more realistic aspirations, only leads to a more punishing round of self-blame and a resolve to drive ourselves harder next time. If we do finally achieve our goals, we are disappointed; despite everything we have done, we still feel empty inside.

• Poor self-esteem makes some of us *afraid* to try. When we undervalue ourselves and our work, we doubt our abilities and are often afraid to ask for the raise or advancement we deserve. If our feelings of self-worth are limited, we place rigid limitations on what we can accomplish. After all, why should we aim for desirable goals when we don't believe we can attain them, or if we do somehow achieve them, don't believe we deserve them?

• We consider ourselves of little importance, both personally and to others. We are excessively demanding when we judge ourselves; too critical of our actions, we continually berate ourselves for real or imagined flaws.

• Vulnerable to the opinions of others, we desperately try to gain their recognition and approval, sometimes through risky and dangerous behavior. Or we may try to impress them by associating with the "right" people, earning the "right" degrees, having the "right" jobs, driving the "right" kind of car, and living in the "right" neighborhood. Our desire for praise and special acknowledgment is endless. Failing to get the recognition we feel should be ours, we become angry and hurt.

• We are at the mercy of our emotions: instead of controlling them, we permit them to control us. Since we allow circumstances to influence our feelings, we are inclined to be moody. The insecurity we feel as a result of devaluing ourselves makes us react with jealousy, envy, and possessiveness. Fear makes us greedy and acquisitive, and feelings of self-hate alternate with those of futility, unhappiness, and depression.

ASPECT TWO: OUR FEELINGS ABOUT LIFE

When we have HIGH self-esteem, *we accept responsibility for, and have a feeling of control over every part of our lives.*

> • We have a comfortable acceptance of reality; we do not blame it for our problems. We set attainable goals and have realistic expectations. We hold ourselves responsible for what occurs in our lives and believe that ultimately, what happens to us occurs primarily because of our choices and decisions, rather than outside factors. Because we acknowledge that *we* are in charge of our lives, we realize we have the power to alter them as we choose. While we are willing to consider others' opinions about how to conduct our lives, we have chosen to be our own final authority, to give the

greatest weight to our own ideas of what is right and best for us.

• The control we exercise is not control over others, or even necessarily over circumstances, but over ourselves and our reactions and responses. We change the circumstances to suit us when it is appropriate and change our attitude about them when it is not.

When we have LOW self-esteem, *our life and what goes on in it often seem out of control.*

• We tend to misrepresent or disregard reality; we overlook some parts of it and over-emphasize others. Sometimes we ignore the world outside us because it feels less real than the world we've created in our heads. Some of us feel so alienated from reality we unwisely choose to put a buffer between it and us with behavior such as excessive smoking, over-eating, alcoholism, or drug addiction. Our thoughts about life are customarily about how badly it treats us and the injustice of the terrible things that happen to us. Instead of directing our thoughts to the world around us, more commonly we egotistically turn them inward toward ourselves.

• We feel powerless, weak, and vulnerable at times, like helpless victims unequal to dealing with even the smallest challenges of daily life. Since we often feel inadequate, unworthy, and inferior, we try to cover up these feelings. In doing so, we sometimes alienate people by appearing prideful and arrogant.

• The control we seek is primarily control over others. Since people are often unwilling to behave as we want them to just for the asking, we try to manipulate them into doing what we want by persuading them to turn their negative emotions against themselves.

ASPECT THREE: OUR RELATIONSHIPS

With HIGH self-esteem, *we have a tolerance of and respect for all people, along with the belief that they are entitled to the same rights we wish for ourselves.*

> • When we are comfortable with ourselves, we respect people's right to be as they are, do as they choose, and live as they see fit, as long as they are willing to extend the same courtesy to us and others. We do not try to force our values or beliefs on people because we don't need their acceptance to make us feel worthwhile.
> • We are reasonable, accepting of others' shortcomings, even-tempered, flexible, and responsible in our relationships. We see all persons as equally worthy and equally deserving of respect. The idea that one person can be inherently more worthwhile than another is inconsistent with the principles of high self-esteem.

When we have LOW self-esteem, *we lack basic respect for others. We are intolerant of people and believe they should live the way we want them to.*

> • We want others to model their behavior after ours because we unconsciously consider their acceptance of our code of conduct as validation of ourselves. Even if others' behavior does not affect us, we sometimes become outraged if it conflicts with our moral standards or the set of rules we live by. Driven by a compulsive need for confirmation, we blame, complain, moralize, and become angry,

intolerant, and bigoted. We are rigid, inflexible, and demanding in our relationships with others.

• We are usually so concerned with ourselves we have little time to think of anything or anyone else. When we do think about people, typically, it is only to wonder what they're thinking about *us*: do they like us, and if not, why not?

• We sabotage our personal relationships. Unsure of ourselves, we frequently feel insecure and uncomfortable around other persons. Instead of being friendly, we act shy and embarrassed or angry and defensive. Since feelings of unworthiness prevent us from enjoying the pleasures of mutually fulfilling relationships, we are often lonely and self-pitying. Ironically, our desire for closeness often results in such possessive behavior on our part that we often drive others away.

• Believing we deserve no better, we enter into relationships with people who reflect our faulty beliefs about ourselves and treat us badly. Since we place a low value on ourselves, they do, too. Some of us let ourselves be abused, verbally or physically. Believing we are by nature bad, we consider such punishment reasonable and justified.

WHAT SELF-ESTEEM IS NOT

Egotism is not High Self-Esteem

Some people confuse high self-esteem with egotism, but the two are vastly different. The ego is a pale imitation of self-esteem; it is an artificial creation that comes into existence to occupy the void which should be filled by genuine good feelings about ourselves. The ego makes us wish for special recognition, to stand out from the crowd. It has an insatiable need for praise; like a bottomless cup, no matter how much is poured into it, there is never enough.

Unlike self-esteem, which allows us to feel good without a specific reason, the ego allows us to feel good only conditionally, "because of" things like possessions, accomplishments, wealth, status, degrees, titles, honors, and so forth. Nothing is wrong with having any of these, but relying on them to make ourselves feel good means we must keep adding to this list or run the risk of feeling *bad*.

Selfishness is not High Self-Esteem

Selfish people are not guilty of loving themselves too much, but too little. While their actions may seem to be caused by excessive self-love, they are actually brought about by feelings of inadequacy and self-doubt. It is true selfish people do not love others, but they love themselves even less.

WHAT WE CAN EXPECT FROM IMPROVING OUR SELF-ESTEEM

Obviously, it's more enjoyable to feel good about ourselves than to feel bad, but aside from this, what benefits can we expect from elevating our self-esteem?

Our Feelings About Ourselves

It is impossible to overstate the importance of high self-esteem because how we feel about ourselves affects everything we do, say, and think. Regardless of the current status of our self-regard, any effort we expend to improve it will bring positive change to our lives. After all, we don't have to actively dislike ourselves in order to want to like ourselves better, nor feel totally wretched before we want to expand our ability to experience happiness.

Our Interaction With the World

The extent of our self-esteem decides whether we see the world as cold, hostile, and uncaring, or warm, loving, and welcoming. When our feelings about ourselves improve, so does the way we perceive reality. We will greet each day eagerly because we find it altogether more pleasant to be alive. As we become more relaxed and more comfortable with ourselves, the pace of life seems to slow, and life itself becomes simpler and less of a struggle.

Our feelings about ourselves determine whether we consider problems overwhelming obstacles or fresh opportunities for growth. The better we like ourselves, the easier we find it to handle life's adversities. With high self-esteem, it's simpler to notice and eliminate our problem-causing behavior; rather than creating difficulties for ourselves, we create personal peace. Instead of being a struggle, life is fun, as it is supposed to be.

Our Relationships

Since our attitude about ourselves determines the quality of our relationships, as we change, so do they. The way we behave toward ourselves tells others how to behave toward us. As we begin to like ourselves better, we notice others' attitudes toward us improve; believing in our personal worth, we unconsciously transmit that message, and others respond by behaving better toward us.

Our relationships become more pleasant, rewarding, and mutually satisfying. By improving our self-esteem, we eliminate many unhelpful traits both we and others dislike. As a result, we are more comfortable around others and they are more at ease around us. When we feel warm and friendly toward ourselves, it is easy to give and receive love freely. The more unqualified love we give others, the more we receive in return.

By understanding our own appraisal of ourselves is more important than how others view us, we eliminate the need to impress them. We become less self-conscious; when people offer us compliments, instead of shrugging them off or feeling embarrassed, we accept them graciously. We no longer become upset when others criticize us; being centered and at peace within ourselves, we accept their criticism comfortably, without wasting time or energy on defending the ego.

High self-esteem makes us comfortably and naturally assertive, less easily taken advantage of, and able to stand up for our rights without being unpleasant. Our new-found independence may cost us some friends, but if it does, it is because they can no longer benefit from our weakness. On the other hand, we will gain new friends who respect us for what we are, instead of what we can do for them.

As we learn more about ourselves, we come to understand others better. We feel more inclined to treat others with kindness, compassion, and respect because regard for ourselves is the basis of caring and respect for others. Inevitably, we will notice beneficial changes in those around us; as we change and become more positive about ourselves, our open and accepting behavior makes positive change easier for them.

Improving Self-Esteem Sets The Stage for Positive Change

Many of us would like to improve our lives and we put a great deal of effort into doing so. Because we give positive change such a high priority, it is important we understand this: *sound self-esteem is the basis for ALL self-improvement;* it is the foundation for any beneficial changes we want to make, in either ourselves or the quality of our experience.

As human beings, our potential is limitless, our abilities inexhaustible, and the possibilities for creative and constructive change are endless. *But,* we won't experience satisfactory progress toward our goals or make any lasting improvements, *unless we believe we deserve the good we want.* Just wanting more out of life is not enough; we must first give ourselves *permission* to have it. If we fail to, then no amount of changes will make us happier.

Regardless of how many wonderful events take place in our lives or how fortunate we are in other ways, unless we believe we deserve to have and enjoy the good that comes our way, it will slip through our fingers, or we will fail to appreciate it because we don't believe we genuinely merit it. Conditions in our lives, whether related to finances, occupation, relationships, or anything else, will improve permanently *only* when we believe we are entitled to something better. If we don't believe we deserve to better ourselves, then making changes will only increase our frustration. Remember: *the first step toward improving our lives outwardly is improving our self-esteem inwardly.*

* * *

3

Why We Have Poor Self-Esteem

HOW IT ALL BEGAN

When we came into this world as babies, it was with a clean slate, so to speak. We knew absolutely nothing about ourselves, either good *or* bad. Since, in our unself-conscious state, we had no reasons to dislike ourselves, we automatically had high self-esteem. This state of blissful ignorance, however, was only temporary. Like tiny sponges, our minds soon began to soak up information about ourselves from our parents and our environment. With the input we received, we began fashioning the self-image that would follow us into our adult life.

Children fortunate enough to have parents with high self-esteem learn to love and accept themselves without reservation. In doing so, they establish a solid experiential basis for their own high self-esteem. Sadly, too few of us were brought up in such advantageous circumstances. Instead, the majority of us were raised by caregivers and authority figures who, themselves, had inadequate self-esteem, persons who had learned unrealistic, impractical thought and behavior patterns from *their* parents. Unwittingly, they passed their incorrect beliefs, values, and concepts on to us by way of their attitudes, feelings, and actions.

We may feel tempted to blame those who parented us for the sad state of our feelings of self-worth, but this would be unjust. They did not intentionally set out to make us feel unworthy. In truth, they were as much victims of the system as we were. Like us, they were brought up by people who didn't like themselves enough. And people who do *not* like themselves don't know how to raise children who *do*; we cannot teach what we do not know. Our parents did the best job they could — *with the resources available to them.* It was not their fault those resources were so limited and inaccurate. But since they were, all our parents could do was pass on the unhealthy, faulty concepts and ideas *they* had accepted in good faith. Like family traditions, the feelings of inadequacy, unworthiness, and insecurity *they* had inherited were handed down to us.

We Learned Love Was Conditional

Since we seldom received love for being just as we were, it was impressed on us that we were not essentially lovable. Love, we discovered, was a commodity dispensed in exchange for something else, much like a business transaction. Our parents were willing to give us their love only if we earned it by following certain rules and meeting specific conditions: we were lovable only *if* we got good grades; *if* we stayed out of trouble; *if* we did as we were told; *if* we kept our room clean; *if* we worked hard; *if* we chose the right friends; *if* we did the thousand and one things they expected of us. If we failed to meet their demands, they withheld their love and acceptance.

We Learned to Feel Insecure

Insecure people are unlikely to encourage genuine feelings of security in their children. They are more likely, because of either ignorance or a desire to share their own misery, to foster feelings of deficiency and inadequacy in those in their care. As a result, we learned we should be apprehensive about tomorrow and to expect the worst because that was what we would probably get. We were warned not to get our hopes up too high or to plan for the future because hardly anything works out the way we expect it to, unless we anticipate it working out badly. We acquired the belief that the world was not a pleasant place to live because pain and worry were destined to be our constant companions. Life, we were told, was meant to be endured, not enjoyed.

We Learned to Feel Inadequate

Sometimes we were made to feel inferior by being compared with other persons who were superior to us in certain ways. Why, we were asked, weren't we as bright, talented, or industrious as their friends' children? Why couldn't we be as well-behaved as the child next door, who was always so nice and polite? Why didn't we get all A's on our report card, like our older sister or brother? Why hadn't we worked harder in school, so we could have gotten a scholarship like our cousin?

By emphasizing our shortcomings instead of complimenting us on our strengths, our parents led us to believe there was something seriously wrong with us. Over a period of time, their negative comparisons made it appear inevitable that no matter how hard we tried, we would never successfully measure up to others. Regardless of how highly-skilled and accomplished we might be today, we habitually think of ourselves as "not quite good enough."

Through comparisons, many of us learned we were stupid, ignorant, wicked, ugly, fat, pathetic, or sloppy. Or, we were careless, lazy, clumsy, dumb, foolish, hopeless, or almost any other unflattering term. Consequently, we grew up with a lot of negative labels attached to us. Eventually our parents' criticisms became so familiar we began to think of them as our own.

School Left Its Mark

It would have been hard enough on our self-esteem if we had received this kind of treatment only at home. For many of us, though, it continued even after we walked out the door in the morning. Our classmates and teachers, themselves usually victims of faulty self-esteem, frequently tried to diminish *their* feelings of unworthiness by increasing *ours*. Also, rather than teaching us to reason independently so we could develop our thinking skills, school taught us to be dependent on authorities.

The competitive framework within which classroom and school activities are commonly designed provided continual opportunities to prove we were losers, further diminishing our already-low feelings of self-worth. And since one of the consequences of passing through our educational system is that we come to believe fitting in with others is important, we also learned to hide our individuality under a mask of conformity.

Social Codes Lowered Our Self-Esteem

We were taught many unworkable social rules as we grew up, principles we were expected to follow in our relationships. Since people were sometimes hurt by others' actions, we were told we must go out of our way to avoid upsetting anyone, even by accident. Because others' opinions of us were important, we learned we must do whatever was necessary to insure they thought well of us. It was best, we found, to be obedient, to follow rules, and not to question authority, or we might draw unfavorable attention to ourselves.

Accepting these and equally irrational ideas guaranteed us a further drop in self-esteem. All of them, without exception, are based on the assumption that others are either more important or more intelligent than we are. Too, the impractical and unrealistic nature of these precepts often makes following them impossible or undesirable. Not understanding this, when we fail to comply with them, as we often must, we unwisely accept the blame and consider ourselves hopeless bunglers.

We Developed Unrealistic Expectations

To make the situation still worse, we were encouraged to have unreasonable expectations of life, to hope for things unlikely to happen. Based on the examples of those around us, we were led to believe life or God owed us certain things, and we should be disappointed, unhappy, or angry if we failed to get them. While popular songs glorified the painful negative emotions they told us were to be expected, romance novels informed us we could live happily ever after despite them. Immersed in the heady unreality of daily television, we learned that most problems could be resolved in half an hour, and sports heroes and media stars were demi-gods deserving of our respect and adoration.

We Learned to Defer to "Experts"

Based on our parents' example, we assumed we were too inept or incapable to handle certain aspects of our lives ourselves. Consequently, we turned over all responsibility for them to persons supposedly better qualified to handle them than we were. As a result, we allowed such highly personal matters as religion and physical and psychological health to be taken from our hands and placed in those of professionals, effectively reducing our control over our lives. Since specialists were willing to relieve us of these responsibilities, we were told, there was no reason we should undertake the difficult, confusing job of investigating them ourselves.

Why We Don't Challenge These Beliefs

Why didn't we dispute these beliefs? Because as children, we were understandably gullible. Young, naive, inexperienced, and impressionable, we were too lacking in knowledge and judgement to tell the difference between truth and fiction and too dependent to challenge it even if we had. Since our parents seemed god-like and infallible to us then, we trustingly accepted their opinions as facts. After all, they were responsible for our well-being, and if they cared enough to look after us, surely we could depend on them to tell us the truth.

As we grew older, we became less accepting of what our parents said, but more receptive to misguided and immature ideas of friends and classmates. By the time we reached adulthood, we were thoroughly indoctrinated with the unhealthy values and the illogical, negative beliefs (often referred to as conventional wisdom) which result in low self-esteem. As adults, we don't dispute these ideas simply because it doesn't occur to us to do so. So thoroughly have we been socialized with these inaccurate concepts that it does not enter our minds there could *be* any acceptable alternatives.

But even should we feel inclined to question these self-esteem-lowering concepts, our belief in their correctness is continually reinforced and reaffirmed by friends, family members, and associates, all of whom have themselves absorbed and accepted much of the same erroneous information *we* have. We are so steeped in conformity we are *afraid* to dispute these ideas, fearful doing so would only add to our difficulties by making others think we were different or "strange." At this point, low self-esteem not only feels natural, it has become our customary way of life.

THE CORE BELIEFS OF LOW SELF-ESTEEM

What was the ultimate outcome of this kind of upbringing? How did having this negativity and unreality continually directed our way for years affect us? The answer, unfortunately, is all too predictable. As a result of it, we came to have primarily a negative view of ourselves, or to put it another way, we developed delusions of inadequacy. As Dr. Eric Berne once put it, "We are born princes and the civilizing process turns us into frogs." Based on our childhood experiences and on the incorrect and unworkable beliefs and ideas we absorbed, we reached three damaging conclusions about ourselves:

1) **We have little control over our lives; we are victims to whom things just happen.**
2) **We are inadequate, incapable, and dependent; we often fail at ordinary things; we will never measure up to others.**
3) **We are essentially bad and wicked; there is something basically wrong with us; we deserve to be punished.**

To one degree or another, all of us with poor self-esteem accepted these self-defeating beliefs. With them to shape our thinking and our lives, we innocently entered the world of adults. We have disguised these destructive beliefs to make them more tolerable because hardly any of us could consciously think so poorly of ourselves and still function effectively in the day-to-day world. No matter how we have obscured these beliefs, they continue to work quietly in the background of our lives, influencing our decisions and condemning us to endless cycles of fear and unhappiness.

That is why, just when life seems to be going well, we "accidentally" sabotage things for ourselves and end up feeling miserable. And why, just when we believe we have found the right person with whom to spend our life, the relationship begins to sour. These beliefs are the mental barriers that make us fail to get what we want from life or, if we do get it, keep us from enjoying it. They are the reason we permit others to take advantage of us and not fight back. They are why we see ourselves as inferior, unworthy, and unlikable. Too, they are the reason we are, to one degree or another, self-centered, unrealistic, and emotionally negative.

RECLAIMING OUR SENSE OF SELF-WORTH

Our Beliefs Are The Problem

Just as we unconsciously picked up our parents' patterns of speech, we unknowingly picked up their habits of thought. Whenever they made a value judgement of us, such as telling us we were smart or dumb, or cute or ugly, or graceful or clumsy, we often agreed with them, because we didn't know any better. Once they labeled us and we accepted it, we began to validate that label, making it a causative factor for our behavior. In this manner, our parents' expectations of us often became our *own* expectations, and our lives became a series of destructive self-fulfilling prophecies.

Although we see what goes on around us each day, we do not look at it objectively; we tend to search out information supporting what we already believe and overlook information calling our beliefs into question. When we think we are unlovable, for instance, we act unlovingly toward ourselves and ignore any evidence suggesting we are not. Other persons, because they tend to treat us as we treat ourselves, often behave badly toward us. If we are unaware of the part we played in causing their reactions, we interpret their behavior as further proof that we are unlovable.

Believing we are inadequate, we seek out situations which allow us to prove it. When we fail in those situations, as we inevitably do, we see our lack of success as confirmation of our judgement of inadequacy. When we *do* perform tasks well, we downplay their significance and belittle our accomplishments. This diminishes our achievements in our eyes and permits us to keep the status of the lowest of the low. In this manner, we proceed through life believing certain ideas are true because evidence we have manufactured ourselves provides the proof!

Our Beliefs Are Powerful

Is it possible for beliefs to affect us so greatly? Do they actually have the power to alter the course of our lives? There is no question about it. When we believe something is true, it makes no difference whether it is or not; as long as we *believe* it is, *we behave as though it is.*

In many respects, our mind is much like a computer and our beliefs like the programs that run it. Just as computers sometimes have problems because of badly-written programs, so do our minds. Computer programmers and users sometimes employ the abbreviation *GIGO*, which is an acronym for the phrase, *garbage in, garbage out.* GIGO is used in connection with situations where, because we are either using a poorly-written program or have entered incorrect data, we end up with unsatisfactory results. This is the position we are in now; we are unhappy with our lives because we have been running our minds with "garbage" beliefs.

IT'S TIME FOR A CHANGE

Our problem does not lie in any genuine imperfections; we are all right exactly as we are. The truth is, **we have low self-esteem only because we believe a lot of things that aren't true!** As Ernest Holmes, founder of the Church of Religious Science said, "Change your thoughts, change your life." Since we have low self-esteem because of certain beliefs (i.e., our thoughts), the way to change the situation is to change those beliefs. This is easier than we might think because the beliefs which make us think poorly of ourselves are *wrong*, every one of them! **We have *no* legitimate reasons to dislike ourselves and, consequently, no reason to have inadequate self-esteem.**

Some people would have us believe we must fill our heads with good thoughts about ourselves to acquire high self-esteem. This is known as the "additive approach," which assumes our minds are like empty vessels just waiting to be filled. The problem, however, is not that our minds have nothing in them — it is that they have been filled with a particularly poisonous kind of information. Consequently, we can achieve high self-esteem by *letting go* of the harmful, incorrect beliefs that keep us from experiencing it.

Our problem is not one of learning to love ourselves more, but of disliking ourselves *less*. We don't have to *create* high self-esteem in ourselves, because it is our natural state. As we eliminate the beliefs that harm us, our natural good feelings about ourselves come to the surface. It's like holding a cork under water; when we release it and it is free of the pressure holding it down, it shoots effortlessly to the top. The same is true of our feelings about ourselves; once we are rid of the erroneous ideas that cause poor self-esteem, we will automatically like ourselves because we will have no reason not to!

We do not have to become perfect to reclaim our self-esteem; we just need the courage to challenge the beliefs that make us think poorly of ourselves. When our minds are free of these beliefs, we will be open to a more joyous, more satisfying way of life. Reclaiming your self-esteem is like suddenly remembering you have a million dollars in your bank account, when you have been worrying about finding enough money for next month's rent.

If we put forth the effort to throw off the crushing burden of self-directed negativity that has weighed us down for so long, we will make a wonderful discovery:

Like the ugly duckling, there is a swan hidden inside all of us.

> "Not to imitate, but to discover — *that* is education, is it not? It is very easy to conform to what your society or your parents and teachers tell you. That is a safe and easy way of existing; but that is not living, because in it there is fear, decay, and death. To live is to find out for yourself what is true..."
>
> J. Krishnamurti

* * *

4

Making Changes

"Change is natural and wholesome, not something to fear and avoid. By looking carefully at the changes that have happened in our lives, we can see that the process of change is what brings all good things about. When we allow ourselves to change, life swiftly carries us past difficult times and into times of joy and vitality."
TARTHANG TULKU

What can we do to improve our opinion of ourselves? This chapter contains information to acquaint us with *affirmation* and *visualization*, two powerful techniques to effectively help us replace negative life patterns with beneficial ones. Armed with these procedures, we will be ready to start the journey to improved self-esteem.

AFFIRMATIONS

What Are Affirmations?

Affirmations are sentences or statements we repeat over and over with the intention of convincing ourselves they are true. We can say them out loud, in our minds, or both. There is nothing mysterious about them; they work on sound psychological principles to help change and improve our lives.

Nor is there anything startlingly new about affirmations; we all use them, and have for years. If we think about it, we will realize there is usually a continual stream of chatter going on inside our heads, as we carry on mental conversations with ourselves. Everyone does this. Talking to ourselves like this is sometimes referred to as *self-talk*, or *mind-talk*. Unfortunately, much of what we tell ourselves *about* ourselves is negative. We say things such as, "I can't do it," "I'm so ugly," "I'm a slob," "I'm too old," "Nobody likes me," "I'm dumb," "I get all the unlucky breaks," "I can't do anything right," and so forth. Continued repetition of these harmful messages keeps our self-esteem low and adds to the hostile, pessimistic feelings we have about ourselves.   From here on out we will reverse this practice and use affirmations to our benefit, to help us learn the positive truths about ourselves we should have absorbed when we were young. We will substitute constructive, self-enhancing mind-talk for the negative, harmful, self-defeating mind-talk we have directed at ourselves in the past.

When to Use Affirmations

One of the best times to put affirmations to work is when we notice we are putting ourselves down. Too many of us have the habit of directing damaging, hurtful, and generally untrue, accusations at ourselves. From now on, the instant we become aware we are doing this, let us make it a point to counterattack with positive self-statements, to cancel out the effects of those that are negative.

There are many times during the day when we can put affirmations to work. We can repeat them while we are riding the bus, during our lunch hour or coffee-break, while waiting for an appointment, when doing housework or any other task which does not demand our full attention. It is good to go to sleep repeating affirmations and to wake up with one in our mind first thing in the morning.

Some people benefit from writing each affirmation down on paper at intervals during the day. This is sort of a double-barreled approach because we are both reading and writing (and possibly even speaking) them at the same time. This usually has the effect of intensifying our concentration, which makes the powerful messages in our affirmations sink in even deeper.

We may find it useful to write affirmations on something we can carry with us, like a small card to fit into our shirt pocket or bag. This can be especially handy when we are just starting to memorize new, positive statements. Another advantage to carrying them with us is we always have something to do if we get stuck in bumper-to-bumper traffic, have to wait for a bus, or become involved in any kind of situation where we would otherwise end up wasting our time.

At this point, you may be wondering if you will have to go through the rest of your life dragging shoe boxes full of affirmations around just to keep your self-esteem intact. Definitely not. After you work on positive self-statements for a certain length of time, they become assimilated into your belief system and you no longer have to think of them.

The Two Kinds of Belief

There are two different ways we "believe" things; the first is when we absolutely *know* something to be a fact. Prior experience, for example, has made us believe the law of gravity is a reality, and if we ignored it, we would plummet to the earth if we stepped off the top of a skyscraper. Or we believe fire is hot, so we know better than to put our hand on the burner of a stove. Beliefs like these are based on demonstrable facts; we can prove their truth to ourselves if we are willing to risk the possible consequences.

The other kind of beliefs are those we have accepted intellectually but have not yet put into practice. We may say we believe honesty is the best policy, for instance. But unless we are scrupulously honest in all our dealings, it is more accurate to say we *accepted it in principle*, which, as Otto von Bismarck once pointed out, means we do not have the slightest intention of carrying it out.

Affirmations work because a principle psychologists refer to as *cognitive dissonance* tends to narrow the gap between these two kinds of beliefs. Usually, if a new idea conflicts with one that is long-held, we tuck the new one away in the back of our mind and do not actually behave as if it were true. Sooner or later, though, we may drag it out of mothballs, refresh our thinking about it, and compare it once again with our current one. Each time we look at both ideas objectively, the new idea gains more strength, and the old one loses some. Because affirmations continually make us compare conflicting beliefs, they tend to speed up the process, until the way we want matters to be becomes the way they are.

Why Affirmations Are Effective

The chief purpose of affirmations is to remind us of new truths we have chosen to become permanent parts of our life. At first these ideas will be a part of only our waking consciousness, but after a period of time, they become a permanent part of our belief system.

Once we accept a new belief as true, it has an immediate impact on our lives. The more we think about it, the greater its effect. As we repeat affirmations, they continually remind us of situations or conditions we wish to create. And because anything to which we give a great deal of thought becomes more real to us, the more we think about them, the more real they become.

How Affirmations Work

To give you an example of how affirmations work, let's say you are inclined to back down whenever anyone disagrees with you, even when you know you're right. So you adopt as your affirmation, "I have the courage to support my convictions." If you make a point of repeating this a number of times each day, over a period of time you will find yourself thinking about it more and more. As you do, the idea becomes more believable to you. With continued repetition, your belief-in-principle becomes your belief-in-fact, and you feel comfortable expressing and supporting your convictions, even if others disagree with you.

Creating Affirmations

You will probably find some affirmations in this book "fit" better than others. Use those you like best or make up your own if you're more comfortable with them. If you want to create your own, here are some general guidelines to help:

> 1) If possible, avoid using negative or derogatory terms and phrases. Keep your affirmations positive and life-enhancing;
>
> 2) Resist the urge to make affirmations about others' behavior. The only changes we are responsible for are those we make to ourselves. If we try to include others in the process of change, we will probably frustrate ourselves and irritate them;
>
> 3) Try to keep your affirmations comfortably short. Those so long we have difficulty remembering them are usually less effective. When we are concerned with trying to recall an affirmation, it is hard to keep our mind on its meaning;
>
> 4) Keep your affirmations in the present tense. Instead of saying "I will forgive myself for my mistakes," say, "I forgive myself for my mistakes." If we phrase affirmations in the future, we may postpone realizing them indefinitely.

VISUALIZATION

What Is Visualization?

Visualization is the process of using our imagination to create realistic mental pictures of behavior we would like to adopt and then regularly focusing our attention on these pictures until we manifest them. So, if we want to replace our customary response to certain situations with actions we consider more helpful, visualization is a useful tool to help make the change.

The technique of visualization is not a new one — public speakers have used it for years, imagining they were facing an audience as they practiced their speeches. A continually increasing number of athletes are using it as a regular part of their training because they attain greater levels of skill than they can with just ordinary practice. Visualization is being used effectively in medical settings, to reduce and eliminate tumors, to lower blood pressure, and to speed and improve healing. In the cognitive-behavioral area of psychology, it is being used successfully to help people reduce stress and stress-related problems, to stop smoking, and to eliminate other self-defeating behavior.

Nothing about this procedure is strange or odd; all of us have employed it numerous times to create mental blueprints for our future. Unfortunately, we were probably unaware of the significance of what we were doing. As a result, the pictures we created may have done more to harm us than to help.

Visualization Is Important

Until we make a conscious decision to change specific aspects of our behavior, we will be unconsciously driven by past programming. Whatever actions we perform will be done, not because we have intentionally *chosen* to do them, but because others have programmed us to. Using visualization, we can assume an active part in directing our future; instead of allowing people and circumstances to control our lives, we can do our own programming and *consciously* direct our actions.

Using Visualization

Here are the steps for using this technique:

> 1) Decide what behavior you want to change and then create a mental pattern of exactly how you want to act in a particular situation. Take your time with this step and be sure you are completely satisfied with your efforts. In some cases, you may even want to take several days to work it out. Postpone visualizing your new actions until you are certain they are what you want. You may find it helpful to write down each part of your visualization, item by item, to make it easier to remember.

2) Ideally, this part of the procedure should be done in a quiet place where you will be uninterrupted. If this is impossible, find the quietest place where you are least likely to be interrupted. Make yourself comfortable, either by sitting or lying down. Consciously relax your body as deeply as possible, so you can give your full attention to the mental pictures you are going to create. Take several slow, deep, breaths, relaxing more with each breath.

3) When you are comfortable and relaxed, imagine yourself performing the new behavior exactly as you want it. If other persons are involved in your visualization, make them so real in your imagination it is as if they are there with you. Feel the emotions you'll feel when your visualization becomes reality; let your body resonate with their physical sensations. If conversation is involved, mentally speak the words you would say. Embellish your mental picture with every detail you can think of, making it as real and as complete as if it were actually happening.

4) When you have finished, relax a few moments longer, holding on to the emotions and sensations as long as you can.

5) Repeat steps 1 — 4, two or three times each day if possible, until you feel so comfortable with your new behavior you are ready to use it.

Theoretical Considerations

Establishing new behavior patterns using these techniques may seem artificial, but bear this in mind: considering the immense variety of actions we perform, comparatively few are instinctive. To a large extent, we learned our patterns of behavior by copying the actions of others. When we use visualization to train ourselves with alternate behavior, we are deciding for *ourselves* what we want to do, instead of borrowing a set of actions from another.

Our new behavior may feel strange and out of character, not at all like our usual selves. That is the whole point of this exercise. Since we are trying to replace old behavior with some we believe will work more to our advantage, it *should* feel different and strange. If we feel out of character, it is because we are; we are trying to create a *new* character, not stick with the same one that so often made us unhappy. As far as any discomfort is concerned, although we have probably forgotten about it, *every* behavior pattern we have ever learned felt uncomfortable until we became used to it (think about learning to tie your shoes as a child!). But **any behavior that is repeated often enough eventually becomes comfortable.**

Why Visualization Works

When we vividly imagine ourselves performing a particular action, our bodies and minds respond much like they would if we actually *were* doing it. After a certain amount of practice, we become so comfortable with the idea of performing the action that when the time arrives for our real-world performance, it happens easily and naturally. If we try to make changes without preparing for them with visualization and affirmation, we are likely to fall back into our old, unhelpful behavior patterns. Visualization, we might say, is rehearsal for a part we wish to perform on a permanent basis.

There are other reasons visualization and affirmation work. First, they force us to clearly identify what we want. Too often we know we want our lives to improve, but because we don't know where to start, we don't start at all. The more clearly we identify the changes we wish to make, the quicker we will make them reality. Second, we often fail to achieve realistic goals because we don't believe we deserve them. With the help of affirmations and visualization we gradually convince ourselves it is all right to have what we want. Once we decide it is OK to have something, we open ourselves up to ways to get it or to make it happen.

IMPORTANT POINTS ABOUT
AFFIRMATION AND VISUALIZATION

Let's Not Rush Things!

We will usually find it best to start small and work our way up to bigger projects. If we have been shy and quiet for years, it would be unbelievable to those we know (including ourselves) if we were to become a "blockbuster" personality overnight. Another advantage to starting small is that our ability to use visualization improves with time and practice.

Be Realistic

To be effective, affirmations and visualizations should be based on believable, attainable, ideals, on reasonable and humanly possible goals. Affirming daily that you can fly is unlikely to get you off the ground unless you arrive at the airport with an airline ticket in hand. Visualizing yourself as the potentate of an oil-rich Arab state will do you little good unless you happen to be next in line for the throne. Avoid the realm of fantasy; aim for goals grounded firmly in reality.

Change Is Not an Overnight Process

When we decide to make changes in our lives, we may be tempted to expect an immediate remodeling. This is unrealistic. Since it took years to get *into* our present condition, it would be unreasonable to demand a total reversal of harmful thought patterns overnight. We must allow time for our new beliefs and behavior to become integrated with the others we have.

Now that we are armed with methods to make important and necessary changes in our self-esteem, it is time to move on to **Part Two.**

* * *

PART II

BELIEFS THAT AFFECT OUR SELF-ESTEEM

5

Accepting Ourselves

"There are things about ourselves that we need to get rid of; there are things we need to change. But at the same time, we do not need to be too desperate, too ruthless, too combative. ...many of those things will change themselves, and the others can be worked on as we go."
BENJAMIN HOFF

*M*ISTAKEN BELIEF:

There are many things wrong with me and so many ways in which I do not measure up to others that I am of little value as a human being.

We find it extremely difficult to accept ourselves just as we are; we are too critical and too demanding. We take ourselves so seriously that instead of laughing about our mistakes, we feel humiliated. Errors we willingly overlook in others seem unforgivable when we make them ourselves. We are by turns, angry, embarrassed, horrified, guilty, and shamed by what we do. Just what is it we believe is wrong with us? Why are we so hard on ourselves? Are we as awful as we think, or could it be we are just looking at matters the wrong way?

WE MAKE PROBLEMS
SEEM WORSE THAN THEY ARE

We Try to Imagine How We Look to Others

Among the biggest obstacles to self-acceptance is our continual effort to imagine how we must appear to others. Believing it is important to maintain a certain kind of image and make a favorable impression, our over-concern with others' opinions makes us exaggerate our problems and enlarge them out of proportion. Sometimes we work ourselves into a frenzy trying to imagine exactly what people are thinking about something we have done or said.

What a waste of time and energy! Few things are more futile than trying to guess how others view us. When we are tempted to, there are some questions we need to ask ourselves. Are their opinions more important than our own? Of course not, and if we believe they are, we think more highly of them than of ourselves. Are others' thoughts about us actually of such consequence we need worry about them? Not unless they have something we want, and they must think well of us before we can get it. Are others' beliefs about us likely to be more accurate and more factual than our own? Probably not, because their view of reality is as biased as ours, only in different ways.

Concern with others' opinions is unproductive: it offers no rewards, but plenty of anguish. In trying to imagine how others see our faults, we magnify them way out of proportion and make them seem far more important than they could conceivably be. While we are busily trying to imagine what others think about us, they may well be wondering just what *we* think of *them*.

We Think Our Problems Are Unique

We have convinced ourselves our faults and flaws are unique: that we are in some way worse, or worse off than others, that no one else understands just what we are going through. Despite its misleading resemblance to humility, this idea is actually just a particularly deceptive form of egotism. In truth, our problems are not at all unique; they are as ordinary as the common cold. It is only because we are less familiar with others' thoughts than with our own that we believe we suffer alone. For the most part, other people are just like us; they have the same kinds of needs and desires. Since they do, they are likely to have the same kinds of experiences and problems we do. If our difficulties seem unique it is probably because we spend too much time thinking about them.

We Blame Ourselves Too Much

When our self-esteem is low, we may blame ourselves for everything, even for just being ourselves. If problems occur in a relationship, for instance, instead of realizing others may have played a part in creating them, we accept that we are at fault. If the others in the relationship are persons whose own self-esteem keeps them from admitting they are wrong, they are only too happy to let us accept the blame and reinforce our belief that it is all our fault. If this distorted thinking style becomes habitual, we end up apologizing for anything and everything, including our existence.

To give you a personal illustration, while talking with a friend one morning, I found myself disagreeing with him frequently. He noticed too, and angrily accused me of disagreeing with everything he said. Chastened, I realized I had been. Just as I was getting ready to apologize, I had a flash of insight: it *was* true that by expressing contrary views I had disagreed with him. However, that was no reason to feel guilty — it was my *right* to have opposing views. If there were any guilt involved in disagreeing, then he was as guilty as I was for holding views contrary to mine! While accepting blame in situations like this may temporarily ease the pressure, it perpetuates problems, rather than solves them.

Our Inner Critic

At times it seems like there is another person living inside us, a constant companion who continually comments on everything we do. It is not the "still, small voice" that guides and inspires us, but a loud, complaining voice, one that is negative, judgmental, and condemning. Because this voice indulges in fault-finding so much of the time, we can call it our *inner critic*.

Our inner critic has no real existence, of course; we are only talking to ourselves. But when we talk to ourselves as the inner critic, the thoughts we express are not our own, but those of authority figures from our childhood. The criticisms we hear from it may originally have come from a perfectionistic parent, a too-demanding teacher, or an over-zealous minister. For the majority of us, our inner critic is a composite of people. Whatever its source, until we become aware of its destructive effect on us, we are inclined to accept its criticisms as valid. By replaying these voices from the past, our inner critic has created a set of impossible standards, unattainable ideals, and unreasonable demands for perfection. When we fail to live up to them (as we often must, due to their unrealistic nature), the inner critic eagerly points out how, where, and when we went wrong and then tells us how imperfect and stupid we are.

The inner critic is on duty twenty-four hours a day, busily attacking our belief in our abilities and undermining any feelings of worth we have. At its prompting, our weaknesses assume massive proportions and our strengths shrink to insignificance. Sometimes it comments negatively or sarcastically on our efforts and at other times discourages us from even trying.

At times the critic's nagging voice grows quieter and actually seems considerate of our welfare. Typically, this happens when it is warning us against doing something we have been thinking about. The inner critic keeps us from expanding our abilities by cautioning us to be careful, to not reach too high lest we fail and become unhappy. By pointing out that we have failed in the past and suggesting we are likely to do so in the future, it tries to convince us it might be better to not even make the effort. That way we will save ourselves a lot of disappointment.

This harmful inner voice constantly reminds us we don't measure up — we aren't good enough now, and we won't be — ever. Every time we acknowledge its criticism as valid, we add to its strength and lessen the possibility of accepting ourselves as we truly are. With the inner critic as our friend, we need no enemies.

WHY WE DON'T LIKE OURSELVES

When our self-esteem is shaky, we exaggerate our every imperfection; anything we believe might be wrong with us or our behavior assumes far greater importance than it deserves. Here are some complaints we have about ourselves, damaging messages from our inner critic that make us feel insecure, uncomfortable, and unlovable.

"I am inferior to other people."

By having others held up as examples when we were young, we developed the *comparison habit,* which means we continually compare ourselves with others and then label ourselves "inferior" because we do not measure up. We look at people and see certain traits, qualities or attributes we like. Then we look at ourselves and feel unhappy because those same desirable characteristics seem to be missing. Based on our real or imagined lack of these features, we consider others to be "more" than we are — smarter, wealthier, more attractive, better liked; we think of ourselves as "less" — not just in those particular areas, but less than them in our value as a person. It is with this kind of reasoning that we prove to ourselves we are inferior.

Whenever one person is compared with another it is obvious *somebody* has to lose, and if we have a poor opinion of ourselves, it will probably be us. Looking at externals, we can always find things others have and we don't, but this is hardly a sign of inferiority. Comparisons of this sort are always invalid because no one is like anyone else. We are unique individuals with widely varying strengths and weaknesses. Because we are so different from each other, comparing one person with another is an apples/oranges comparison, rather than apples/apples.

Is there any point in comparing ourselves with anyone else? Of course not — life is not a contest; how well we measure up to others is unimportant. What *is* important is stopping this damaging habit. To do so, we need to remember no matter what basis we use for comparison, invariably, some people will seem better than we are, and others will seem worse. The point to remember is that *no one in the world is superior to us in intrinsic worth;* we are all equally worthwhile and valuable.

"Some people dislike me, so there must be something wrong with me."

Sometimes people criticize or ignore us, or do even worse things to show they dislike us. If our self-esteem is low and we are on the receiving end of their displeasure, we interpret their unfriendliness as justification of our bad feelings about ourselves. Mistakenly, we think we and not they are the cause of the problem. Instead of deciding there is something wrong with *them* for disliking us, we let their negative attitude persuade us there is something wrong with *us.*

Trying to change ourselves to make others like us better is not the solution. It is a fact of life that we cannot please everybody, especially those people who enjoy being disagreeable. Generally, though, people dislike us not because of the way we are, but because we remind them of a part of themselves they would rather forget. People only hate something about others when it reflects something they resent about themselves.

Is it important that everybody likes us? Not unless we have entered a popularity competition — we get no bonus points for being well-liked, nor does being liked by a lot of people make us a better person. Speaking realistically, there is no particular reason why everybody should like us, nor, for that matter, why we should like them.

We should be generous enough to allow others the freedom of their own opinion, even if that means they are free to dislike us. As far as some people are concerned, the best way to get along with them is to get along without them.

"I have done such awful things people would want nothing to do with me if they found out about them."

To present a genuinely convincing case against ourselves, it is necessary to produce devastating evidence that clearly demonstrates our innate lack of worth. What could be better than some action of ours we believe would outrage any decent person alive? To reinforce our belief in our basic unworthiness, we periodically recall, with great vividness, certain unwise actions we later came to regret. To accompany these memories, we re-experience the shame, embarrassment, and humiliation we felt then and have felt ever since.

There are, though, two major flaws in this case we have prepared against ourselves. First, people attach different values to the same act; while some people might be horrified by something we'd done, others would simply say, "So what?" Second, we flatter ourselves by believing our secrets are worse or more despicable than anyone else's. With the exception of children too young to act on their own initiative, there is no one alive who does not have guilty secrets and who does not believe his or hers are the absolute worst! None of us has lived such a flawless life that we would care to have every detail of it exposed to the world.

"Something is wrong with the way I look."

Few of us think we look all right the way we are; we believe there is something wrong with the body we are wearing. We inventory each part carefully, cataloging those we consider defective and ignoring the many parts which are perfectly all right. We think we are too tall, too short, too fat, or too thin. Or we believe certain parts of us, like our nose, eyes, feet, teeth, hands, are too big, too small, too long, too wide, too flat, too irregular, or *too* something else. We imagine imperfections where none exist and magnify others way out of proportion. If we could enlarge our income the same way we do our faults and flaws, we would all be living in luxury.

How tall is *too* tall? And how short is *too* short? Using the word "too" is a dead giveaway we are playing the ever-popular Comparison Game; we can not be "too" anything, unless we compare ourselves with someone else. Words like "tall," "short," "beautiful," and "ugly" have no absolute meaning; they are merely terms used to compare one thing with another. Anyone can awaken feelings of inferiority by comparing himself with idealized standards of physical development.

Each of us is unique in physical expression. We need to celebrate that uniqueness, rather than complain about it. If we all looked the same, we would be indistinguishable from everyone else and would simply blend into the crowd. What a painfully dreary world that would be! External differences are unimportant.Regardless of how we look on the outside, on the inside we are all the same.

"I am different from others."

Some of us have been encouraged to believe there is something wrong with us because our ethnic group, language, religion, or skin color is different from the majority of those around us. Or perhaps we grew up in a troubled family, and we believe other persons think less of us because of it. Maybe our sexual orientation is not the same as most others of our gender and we feel different and unacceptable. We may have been brought up in a poor neighborhood or a ghetto and feel this reflects badly on our worthiness. We might have a mental or physical handicap and feel others look down on us.

If any of these factors bother us, it is not because they are important in themselves but because they make us *different* from others. And it is probably others' behavior toward us that made us arrive at the inaccurate conclusion that being unlike them somehow makes us less worthwhile.

This is absolutely false! It is immaterial whether one difference or a thousand sets us apart from others; none of them has the slightest bearing on our value as a person. Our being one way and others being another is unimportant. There are no inherent characteristics, qualities, or attributes that make any one of us better or worse than anyone else. Each of us is unique and valuable as we are — differences and all.

Rather than feeling miserable because we are different from others, we should rejoice, for if we were all alike, life would be intolerably dull. As it is, let us respect our differences and appreciate ourselves for being the unique individuals we are.

"Sometimes my body embarrasses me."

Instead of being something we can depend on for stability, our body sometimes seems to let us down at the worst possible times. It is often unpredictable and on occasions makes noises that humiliate us. Despite the naturalness and inevitability of bodily functions, they sometimes seem so disgusting we dislike even thinking of them. We perspire, we step on people's feet, we trip over things, we spill food on ourselves, we get sick, we have accidents, and we grow older, to name just a few of the problems likely to occur.

Our exasperation, however, is due less to our body's unreliability than to our concern over what others may think of us because of it. We become so wrapped up in our problems we forget others are flesh and blood like we are and are subject to the same kinds of pains and problems. In this respect, we are all alike — to be alive is to be subject to physical limitations. No one, no matter how exalted her title, how high her position, or how wealthy she is, is free from these kinds of occurrences.

"Sometimes I don't understand things and I feel dumb."

At times we have trouble understanding what people tell us. Instead of asking questions (which we believe would make us look stupid), we try to bluff our way through and hope no situation arises to force us to admit we do not know. Sometimes this approach works, and other times it does not. When it does not, we usually end up feeling worse about ourselves than we would have if we had admitted our ignorance in the first place.

Ignorance is not a dirty word or an incurable disease; it is simply a lack of information, a condition easily remedied. Since we are different from one another and because our backgrounds and experiences vary so widely, it is inevitable that sometimes others will appear smarter than we are, and other times we will seem smarter than they are. We cannot realistically expect ourselves to know everything, and there is no point in filling our minds with volumes of information in the hope it will some day be of use.

When we are unable to make sense of what others tell us, we blame ourselves — we think it must be a deficiency on our part that prevents us from understanding them. It is never our fault if we honestly try to understand and fail. We cannot expect to grasp everything told us, regardless of how it is explained; when we are unable to understand something, it is the other person's responsibility to explain it in such a manner that we *can* understand it. It is never wrong to ask questions or admit we do not understand. What *is* wrong is to say we *do* understand when we do not.

"I offend and displease people by doing or saying the wrong thing."

We have acquired a set of unrealistic rules and standards by which we are supposed to regulate our lives. These impractical, idealistic principles come from a number of sources, including our family, friends, teachers, churches, and government. Because their origins are so diverse, instead of working together in a unified manner, they sometimes conflict strongly. The contradictory nature of these precepts makes it impossible to comply with them all because to follow some, we must break others. Despite our best efforts, there will always be some we fail to live up to.

If we take these rules seriously, then every one of us has done things some people might regard as wrong or "sinful." We may as well accept that no matter what we do, how we do it, or how pure our intentions, there will always be someone, somewhere, who may choose to be offended, angered, or hurt by our behavior. To avoid guilt and blame, we need to remember in this context the words "wrong," and "sin" are used primarily by people who, for reasons of their own, want to control our behavior. To keep the proper perspective, we should remember these rules, standards, and ideals exist only in people's *minds*, not in the real world.

"I am not as good, as worthy, or as deserving as others."

Deep inside us we have an overwhelming sense of "not rightness." We know, in our heart of hearts, we are not like others; we are not whole, complete, and perfect like they seem to be. We feel we are not as good, as worthy, as deserving as others; instead, we are bad, wicked, unwholesome, unforgivable, and inadequate. We believe there is something basically wrong with us, or as a young friend of mine once put it, that we are "broken." We feel incomplete — lacking in certain important qualities we think others have.

As a result of these feelings of wrongness, when bad breaks come our way, we accept them hopelessly, thinking they are no worse than we deserve. We are not surprised when circumstances appear to work against us because we believe that is how things work for people like us. No matter how much bad luck seems to dog us, we assume it is inevitable; if we were only more than we were, or better than we are, or a more valuable person, this kind of thing would never happen.

This is possibly the hardest mistaken belief to combat because it is based on "feelings" instead of facts. It's a non-specific sense of unworthiness, a combination of feelings, none of which we can actually put our finger on. We need to confront this belief. Exactly what is it that's missing in us? What are the specific reasons we believe we are unworthy? Why do we think others are better than we are? If we examine the matter closely, we will discover our reasons for this belief are invalid.

We are not insignificant or unworthy or undeserving or without value — we were just made to feel that way when we were too young to know better or to argue the point. So thoroughly have we been convinced we are inferior, that we have neglected to challenge these inaccurate beliefs.

THE TRUTH ABOUT OURSELVES

As far as personal worth is concerned, absolutely *nothing* sets us apart from anyone else. None of these complaints about ourselves make us better or worse than anyone else; they just make us different. There are no criteria by which to measure individual worth. Further, we have no need or obligation to prove our worth to anyone, *including ourselves*; our existence alone is sufficient evidence.

COUNTER-BELIEF:

My value as a human being is unrelated to who or what I am, how I look, what I have done or may do, my race, religion, sexual preference, skin color, my accomplishments or lack of them, my background, or any other factor, including how I compare with others.

Why Self-Acceptance Is So Important

We need to stop being so self-condemning. Criticizing, disliking, or rejecting ourselves for being as we are improves nothing; it just makes it harder to accept ourselves and, consequently, to bring about desirable changes. Let us try a different tactic. Instead of being judgmental, let us acknowledge our faults with sympathy, gentleness, and understanding. Let us also accept that you and I and everyone else in this world are flawed and imperfect people, who rarely make it from one day to the next without making mistakes of one kind or another. Of greatest importance, let us accept that it is perfectly all right to be this way. It is unnecessary to create a "new, improved version" of ourselves like detergent manufacturers do so regularly with their products. All we have to do is accept ourselves, lovingly and unconditionally, faults, flaws, and all.

What does unconditional love and acceptance imply? It means acknowledging the facts about ourselves, without approving or disapproving of them. It means looking at our faults with compassion and understanding. It means being able to accept our imperfections and say, "Yes, I know this is wrong with me, but I like myself anyway." It means forgiveness — letting go of the past so we can do better in the future. It means accepting ourselves totally, no matter how different we are or how we are different. It means saying to ourselves, "This is what I am and who I am, and I am fine just as I am." Finally, it means understanding, with genuine warmth and affection for ourselves, that we are as we are because, for right now at least, we can be no other way.

Accepting ourselves as we are does not necessarily mean we want to *stay* as we are; we may choose to change. If we feel change is necessary, then by all means, let us begin making whatever improvements we think are appropriate, bearing in mind it is easier to change if we do not pressure ourselves to do so. Some changes, we will discover, take place without effort on our part. Interestingly, we will find accepting ourselves lovingly and without conditions is the key to positive change.

*

INCREASING YOUR AWARENESS

1) Draw a line down the center of a sheet of paper. In the left hand column, write something your inner critic has said during the past few days. Repeat the comment to yourself and try to identify its source. You will probably find the majority of your inner critic's remarks came from one particular person from your childhood. After you have determined who made the remark to you originally, write that person's initials in the left margin next to the remark.

Then mentally address your inner critic by name. Challenge its statements. If, for instance, one of your critic's comments is that you never succeed at anything you do, on the right hand side of your work-sheet, opposite the critic's statement, write something like, "That's not true," or, "That's false." Follow this with a list of things at which you *have* succeeded. Your successes needn't be big ones; a lot of us will never paint a Mona Lisa, but we do just fine when it comes to painting our house. *Anything* you've succeeded at, no matter how trivial, will do because it will nullify your inner critic's statement. When you have completed this process for one remark, think of others and follow this same procedure for each of them. Proceed down your list, challenging each comment and writing your rebuttal next to it on the right side of the page.

When you have finished this exercise, save the sheets you have been writing on and put them in your notebook. Then you can refer to them from time to time and add other negative remarks from your inner critic as you become aware of them. You will find just being able to identify the source of these assertions takes away some of their power. The more you work on identifying and rebutting the inner critic's harmful comments, the less they affect you.

Throughout the day, if you notice your inner critic's voice addressing you, call it by name. Talk back to it. Mentally shout at it, if that is helpful. You needn't be polite. Tell it you are wise to its game and refuse to pay it any more attention. After a period of time, your continual defiance and refuting of the inner critic's remarks weakens its power and influence.

2) Sit or lie down in a position where you can be relaxed, comfortable and undisturbed for the next 15 or 20 minutes. Don't become so comfortable, though, that you nod off to sleep. Now close your eyes and begin to notice the thoughts flowing through your mind. Don't initiate any thoughts yourself; just pay close attention to those that occur naturally.

You will find you tend to get sidetracked by getting caught up in your thoughts, instead of just passively observing them. This is inevitable. Don't blame yourself when it happens. Just stop actively thinking, and sit back and resume your observation.

As you watch what passes through your mind, you will be surprised by some of your thoughts; they'll seem petty or mean or vicious or selfish. We have a tendency to try to deny or disown this kind of thought. We have been told it's wrong to entertain such awful ideas, that we should be nicer, and so on. Don't be critical of your thoughts, though, or of yourself for thinking them. This kind of denial is harmful; in denying your thoughts, you deny a part of yourself. Whatever your thoughts, you think them for perfectly logical reasons, so there's no point in telling yourself you should think differently. Give yourself permission to think anything at all, no matter how terrible it might seem, without blaming or judging yourself.

The purpose of this exercise is to develop a non-judgmental attitude toward ourselves. By allowing thoughts to pass through our mind without criticizing ourselves for thinking them, we gradually become more self-accepting. Being able to view our thoughts non-judgementally relieves us of a great deal of pressure and guilt.

AFFIRMATIONS

I do the best and only thing I can do at all times.
I am wonderful and worthwhile just as I am.
It is OK for me to be weak sometimes.
I am as important and worthwhile as anyone else.
I feel warm and loving toward myself.
No one is more or less valuable or worthwhile than I am.
I refuse to call myself derogatory names.
*I accept the facts about myself; they are neither bad nor good; they
    just are.*
I refuse to accept blame, either from myself or others.
I love and appreciate myself just as I am.
I accept my feelings as part of myself.
It is OK to have the feelings I do.
My worth as a person is unrelated to anything about me.
I am whole and complete just as I am.

✳ ✳ ✳

6

Needing Approval

"How much trouble he avoids who does not look to see what his neighbor says or does or thinks, but only to what he does himself."
MARCUS AURELIUS

*M*ISTAKEN BELIEF:

It is important most people love, like, or approve of me.

WE PLACE A HIGH PREMIUM ON BEING LIKED

It is no wonder we believe it important that others regard us favorably; in one way or another, the idea that we should be well-liked has been drilled into us since childhood. Since the truth of this belief seems self-evident, we do not consider it open to question. When people like us, we feel good, and we like ourselves; when they do not like us, neither do we. Our reasoning generally follows these lines:

1) we like to feel good about ourselves;
2) others' favorable opinions of us can make us feel good; therefore
3) it is important they think well of us.

Plus, we know from our own experience that we feel good when others like us. We enjoy people's compliments, even if we believe they are undeserved. We bask in their applause. We relish their appreciation and recognition. We long to be accepted, honored and respected, and by the same token, to avoid being disapproved of, blamed, and rejected. Usually, the higher others' opinions of us, the happier we are.

Despite this intense desire for acceptance, not just anyone's approval will do. For opinions to be important they must be those of people we feel are in some way better than we are, people we can look up to. Approval from persons we consider inferior has little value because we think our judgement is superior to theirs.

Being Liked Has Its Price

On the surface, it seems harmless enough to want people to like us. After all, what is wrong with feeling liked, loved, and appreciated? Not a thing. Nor is there anything inherently wrong with doing things to please others, as long as it pleases us, too. Sometimes, though, we perform services for others strictly because we want their praise and gratitude. Sometimes we have to sacrifice our integrity to get others to like us. When our actions are motivated primarily by a desire to win others' approval, then wanting them to like us is anything but harmless.

DISADVANTAGES OF WANTING OTHERS' APPROVAL

People rarely think highly of us just because we want them to; more than likely, we have to earn their good opinion by behaving in ways they approve of. Consequently, the moment we decide it is important that someone think well of us, we are no longer free to live as we like because we usually gain people's good opinions only in exchange for some of our personal freedom. To the extent we value others' opinions, we put ourselves under their control.

When we consider others' opinions of great importance,

> • *we must be concerned about how people will react to what we say.* Trying to keep people thinking well

of us is like walking on eggs — we must proceed
very cautiously. We have to choose our words
carefully, trying to remember who is offended by
what. Since people might find some of our ideas
objectionable, we are not at liberty to say what we
think. We conceal our true feelings because expressing them may make others think poorly of us.

• *we are required to live by others' rules, standards,
and ideas of right and wrong.* To keep people liking
us, we must often ignore our own wishes and
preferences and modify our behavior to match
their expectations. This means, regardless of how
we feel, we must avoid certain actions because
people disapprove of them and do certain other
things purely because they think we should. In
short, we have to be more concerned with how
people view our behavior than with being ourselves.

• *we must try to create a good impression of ourselves.* To create the right kind of image, we try to
dress fashionably, be seen with the right people,
live in the right neighborhood, drive the right kind
of car, have the right kind of job, and live the right
kind of lifestyle. We make choices as though
people are looking over our shoulder to applaud or
criticize our decisions. We measure the importance
of our achievements, not by their value in *our* eyes,
but by what we imagine others will think of us for
what we have achieved.

• *we are easy to manipulate.* When we place too
much importance on others' opinions, we are easily
trapped into activities we would rather avoid.
Sometimes we are manipulated by people threa-
tening to withhold their approval if we do not do as
they wish, and other times by a pat on the back and
praise for our accomplishments. Because we place
a higher priority on pleasing others than on pleasing

ourselves, we often have to disregard our own feelings and personal needs in favor of theirs. Since some people are exceedingly fussy and demanding, we sometimes put up with a great deal of inconvenience just to keep them liking us.

• *we experience a lot of emotional wear and tear.* Inevitably, concern with others' opinions makes us emotionally vulnerable. Because we give their approval so much weight, we permit their comments to influence our feelings about ourselves. We feel important when others tell us we are and unimportant when they do not. Desiring people's praise makes us susceptible to their blame. Since we feel happy only when people think well of us, when they die or move away or no longer like us, we are in for a stormy time.

• *we feel shy, embarrassed, or self-conscious.* When we consider others' opinions important, we spend a lot of time worrying what they think of our hairstyle, clothing, table manners, driving, behavior, and so forth. This excessive concern is self-defeating. When we are worrying about what people think of us, we are tense and unable to give our full attention to the job at hand. For example, we experience stage fright only because we are more concerned with the impression we are making on the audience than with informing or entertaining them.

WHY WE SEEK EXTERNAL APPROVAL

Clearly, it is not in our best interest to be overly concerned with winning others' approval because attempting to gain it exacts too great a price. Why, then, do we try so desperately to make people like us? As strange as it sounds, we seek others' approval because we disapprove of ourselves.

Healthy self-approval is of prime importance to our continued existence. Without a good opinion of ourselves and the feeling of personal worth it generates, we eventually lose our desire to live. Ideally, we should provide our self-approval directly, but when we like ourselves too little, we are unable to do so. This leaves no alternative but to seek approval from others. Then if *they* like us, we approve of ourselves and develop a feeling of personal worth.

WHY OTHERS' APPROVAL FAILS TO HELP

At first glance, this seems to be a workable solution because when people like us, we *do* feel good about ourselves. However, depending on others' regard has serious shortcomings. First, it is only temporary; it must be continually renewed and replenished. Second, there is never enough to satisfy us; we always want more. Third, although society encourages us to believe others' approval can substitute for our own, it cannot; believing it can is like believing someone else's dinner will provide us with nourishment or that someone else's sleep will make us feel rested.

The most serious consequence of this belief, though, is the damaging effect it has on our self-esteem; by believing others' approval is essential to our self-approval, **we put ourselves in the ridiculous position of having to ask people for permission to like ourselves!** By giving others' approval such importance, we give *them* the responsibility for our self-esteem instead of holding on to it ourselves. We hand our need for approval around like a collection plate on Sunday morning, hoping people will put in enough to take care of our needs. In effect, we say, "Please like me, because unless you do, I won't like myself."

THE TRUTH ABOUT NEEDING APPROVAL

Because we have depended on others' approval to provide us with a feeling of *personal* approval, we have convinced ourselves their good opinions are essential. If we failed to feel adequately approved of, we did whatever we thought would make people like us better, often at great expense to our integrity and human dignity. The good news is, *it has never been necessary to degrade ourselves to win people's good opinions* because there is *no* connection between our personal worth and how people feel about us. Our need is not to get people to like us *better* but to realize, as far as feeling good about ourselves is concerned, they do not *have* to like us at all! It is only *our* approval that matters!

COUNTER-BELIEF:

The only approval I must have is my own; anyone else's is strictly optional.

Don't We Need Love?

Wanting others' approval is such a habit we are inclined to think of it as biological in origin, like our need for food, water, or sleep. Wanting others' validation is acquired behavior, though, not something we are born with. True, evidence shows *children* must receive a certain amount of love and approval to attain normal physical development, but we are adults and, by definition, *are* physically mature. Furthermore, if the need for approval were inborn, everyone would feel it, and there is ample evidence some people do not. Hermits, for instance, live comfortably without others' approval. Some choose to have nothing to do with anyone else. Less radical examples are persons who simply *prefer* solitude, who enjoy being alone without feeling lonely, and who feel no need for others' emotional support. Obviously, the need for approval is not biologically determined, and if we choose to, we can live a happy, fulfilling life with no approval but our own.

The Two Kinds Of Approval

"Wait," you may say, "others' approval is important from the standpoint of survival, isn't it?" It is easier to answer this if we point out there are two kinds of approval.

Practical Approval is essential if we want to be involved in any sort of successful working relationship with others. Without it, we would find it difficult to hold a job, to obtain food and clothing or a place to live, or even to survive. Unless we are prepared to completely turn our back on society and be 100% physically self-reliant, it would be unwise to thumb our noses at others' practical approval.

Personal approval, on the other hand, means others like us as persons, that they approve of us in terms of a personal relationship because we have enough values and standards in common for them to find us acceptable. But unlike practical approval, personal approval is an option. While we may strongly desire it and may feel a certain amount of emotional satisfaction if we get it, it is not a necessity. Because others' good opinions are sometimes the admission price to life's more pleasurable activities, it is often *convenient* to have people like us, and it can even be *preferable* or *desirable*. It is one thing to desire approval so we can feel good and another to want to be approved of so we can have a place to live.

SOLVING THE APPROVAL PROBLEM

Advantages To Not Wanting Others' Approval

There are clear-cut advantages to *not* feeling we must have others' endorsements. When we are overly concerned with others' opinions, we try to persuade people to like us so we can feel good about ourselves. By understanding it is *our* feelings that are important, we eliminate the annoying, and sometimes alienating, compulsion to persuade others to think about us as we wish.

Wanting others' approval makes us dependent. This, in turn, makes us insecure. When we are our own judge, we are not subject to the inconsistencies of others' attitudes; we are neither pleased by their approval nor disappointed by their blame, so we have an abiding sense of security, whether others like us or not.

Whose Opinion **Is** Important?

To reclaim our high self-esteem, we must eliminate the belief that we need others' approval and replace it with a healthy belief in ourselves. We must stop looking outside ourselves to measure our worth and realize that unless approval comes from inside us, it has no lasting value. We must accept responsibility for being the *only* person with the right to approve or disapprove of us. This doesn't mean we must be indifferent to others' opinions. It *does* mean, as we learn to value ourselves, we come to depend on only *ourselves* to provide feelings of self-worth.

What if people *do* disapprove of us? While there is no point in intentionally causing others to think poorly of us, neither is there in altering our behavior to make them like us better. We simply accept they are free to think anything they wish of us, as we are of them. While people are free to offer their opinions of us, we are free to reject them. As long as we do not suffer physical injury or deprivation as a result of people's thoughts, let them be our guests and think what they like. Although the majority of us prefer approval to rejection, we must be prepared to handle either possibility comfortably.

And what if people *are* unkind to us or try to damage our character, or call us nasty names? Then we need to be sure we put our hearts, minds, and energy into approving of ourselves, so no matter what others say or do, we remain untouched and untroubled inside.

*

INCREASING YOUR AWARENESS

1) Do this exercise at the end of your day. Use a sheet of paper from your notebook and leaving the left margin blank, write the name of someone with whom you came in contact today. Skip

two lines, then write in the name of another person with whom you associated today, and skip two more lines. Keep doing this until you have 15 names or run out of people. Now, in the left margin by each name, write the letter **V** if you consider that person's approval Very Important, **S** if you believe it to be Somewhat Important, or **U** if you believe it to be Unimportant. Once you've finished this, start at the top of the list again, and beside every name you've marked with **V** or **S**, write the letter **P** *if that persons' approval is important purely for practical reasons*, such as keeping your job.

Go back to the top of your list. After each name you've marked with either **V** or **S**, but *not* marked with **P**, write what makes you believe this person is superior to you. If you find this difficult to do with the first name, then skip to the second, third, and so on, until you find one more obvious to you. No matter how you skip around, complete this process for every name except those preceded by **P** or **U**. When you have finished, you will have a list of some of the ways in which you believe you are inferior to others.

Now that you have identified some characteristics and traits which make others' opinions of you seem important, keep them in mind whenever you run into any of these people. Suppose, for example, you think John's approval is significant because he is so popular. Then the next time you run into John, say to yourself mentally, "Even though John seems popular, he is no more valuable as a person than I am; his superiority is only in my imagination, not in real life." If you make a habit of doing this, you will find your assessment of these people changing, and the people themselves will appear to change. We use the word *appear* because chances are they will probably be no different than before, but you will start to see them differently.

2) Find a place where you can relax and have privacy for 15 or 20 minutes. Using visualization techniques, create a scenario in which you are with others, and you do something you would ordinarily find embarrassing. It might be easiest to select something that has embarrassed you in the past, like spilling food

on yourself, saying the "wrong" thing, or forgetting someone's name just when you're introducing her to another.

Now, making your mental picture as realistic as possible, imagine yourself in the scene you've created, doing the particular thing you customarily would find embarrassing, *but not reacting to it with embarrassment.* Feel yourself being casual and relaxed, even as others look at you disapprovingly and make judgmental remarks about what you've done. Imagine yourself responding comfortably instead of self-consciously. Mentally tell yourself something like, "Well, everybody makes mistakes; I guess this is one of mine."

Practice this visualization until others' comments and actions lose their sting, and you are no longer inclined to feel uncomfortable in the imaginary situation. When you reach this point, choose a similar set of circumstances and use the same procedure. Continued practice will gradually de-sensitize you to others' opinions.

AFFIRMATIONS

I need only my own approval.
I am free to accept or reject others' opinions about anything, including myself.
I reject any opinion that denies my value as a human being.
People may think anything of me they want; it's my own opinion that's important.
Others' opinions of me are based on their view of reality, not mine.
Regardless of what others think, I am free to think what I choose.
Others' opinions can harm me only if I accept them as true.
I value myself even if others do not.
People don't have to like me.
Except for their practical value, others' opinions are unimportant.
I am thoroughly worthwhile and deserving, regardless of how others feel about me.

Even if others dislike me, I am still a valuable and worthwhile person.

I can do without others' approval, agreement, or validation.

It is unnecessary to impress others with my worth or importance.

Since I am innately worthy, I have no need to boast or try to prove my worth to anyone.

I don't have to please anyone except myself.

* * *

7

Emotional Pain

"We always think our negative emotions are produced by the fault of other people or by the fault of circumstances... Our negative emotions are in ourselves and are produced by ourselves... No negative emotions can be produced by external causes if we do not want it. We have negative emotions because we permit them, justify them, explain them by external causes, and in this way we do not struggle with them."
P. D. OUSPENSKY

"Much of our suffering is useless: it is unknowingly created by us through unenlightened, unintelligent use of our human capacities."
CHARLES T. TART

THE UNIVERSALITY
OF EMOTIONAL DISTRESS

Emotional distress tends to be an all-pervading presence in our lives, as common as eating and sleeping. Depending on the circumstances, we may feel angry, fearful, grief-stricken, hateful, bitter, jealous, hostile, guilty, or any of a number of other painful emotions. An insulting remark from an acquaintance makes us angry; the possibility of losing a job makes us fearful; a close friend moves away, and we are saddened; we are omitted from the guest list for a party, and we feel hurt and rejected; someone else gets the promotion we expected, and we feel hostile, bitter, and resentful.

It is hardly surprising we respond to events like these with negative emotions. From childhood on, we have been surrounded by examples of other persons reacting similarly to their environment. Too many popular songs glorify emotional pain, telling us heartbreak and suffering are inevitable, and we should expect to put up with all kinds of abusive treatment and emotional pain, supposedly in the name of love. The soap operas and romantic fiction flooding the market encourage us to believe emotional anguish and agony are nothing exceptional, just par for the course.

Considering the many incorrect and harmful beliefs about emotion we have absorbed, it is small wonder we are so often upset or depressed. Like our other false beliefs, we have assimilated these so thoroughly they seem like unquestionable facts instead of the unsupported and inaccurate assumptions they actually are.

OUR MISTAKEN BELIEFS ABOUT EMOTIONS

MISTAKEN BELIEF:

I must punish myself with emotional pain when reality is not as I want it to be.

No matter how we look at it, this is undeniably a peculiar belief. Although there is absolutely *no* reason why we should make ourselves feel unhappy when reality turns out to be different from what we wanted, this is exactly what we do. When matters don't go as we hope they will, rather than accept it with a smile, we punish ourselves with painful feelings! If, for instance, we had been anticipating a date with someone special, and at the last minute, the person calls us to cancel it. How do we typically respond? With disappointment, tears, rage, or depression. We beat ourselves up because things aren't the way we want them to be.

COUNTER-BELIEF:

Inflicting pain on myself does not alter reality in the slightest, it just makes the situation worse.

If crying and complaining improved matters they might be worth the effort. But all they do is make us feel worse. When we begin wallowing in self-pity, we lose our perspective and our sense of humor and just become more dejected. This is foolish: is there any sense whatsoever in making ourselves feel bad just because reality is not as we want it to be? Of course not. Besides, making ourselves miserable takes a lot of energy and hard work.

*

MISTAKEN BELIEF:

Emotional pain is normal and inevitable, and I cannot live fully without experiencing it.

We accept emotional pain with a certain amount of fatalism. We hear people express their belief that these negative emotions are natural and that everybody feels them. Since others' behavior appears to bear this out, we accept it as true. Emotional pain *is* normal — in the sense that many or most people experience it. However, since experiencing disturbing emotions is a matter of choice, we can hardly consider it inevitable. To say a course of action is *inevitable* implies there are no alternatives, and there *are* optional ways of responding other than painfully.

Pain is not intended to be anyone's way of life; it is nature's warning device to let us know something is wrong. Its only purpose is to direct our attention to any aspect of our being that needs to be changed. To respond appropriately to pain, we look for its cause, and finding it, eliminate it along with the negative energy it generated. We accept this warning when the pain is physical in nature, so we look for cures or treatments, and we seek relief till we find it. Because we have been conditioned to think emotional pain is unavoidable, rather than trying to remove its cause, we approach it with the idea of learning to tolerate it. However, just as physical pain indicates a physical condition that needs correction, emotional pain points to errors in thinking and urges us to correct them. Obviously, then, we *can* eliminate emotional pain by changing our thoughts about whatever is troubling us.

Counter-belief:

Emotional pain is not inevitable, it is optional, and I can choose not to experience it.

*

Mistaken belief:

My emotional responses are natural and instinctive.

It is tempting to think our negative emotional responses are part of some sort of "package" issued to us at birth, which we had no choice but to accept. But except for the emotions nature gave us to protect ourselves from physical threats, this is not the case. Just as we learned to talk by modeling others' speech, we developed emotional responses by modeling others' behavior.

Although we may have been exposed to a number of different ways we *could* respond to a given situation, generally, we adopted the responses which produced what we considered the most desirable results. Once selected, we tended to go on using them whenever a similar situation occurred. With repetition, these harmful emotional responses came to feel "automatic." Today we think of them as fixed and inflexible, instead of as the habits they actually are.

COUNTER-BELIEF:

My negative emotional responses are neither natural nor instinctive; I copied them from others as I was growing up.

*

MISTAKEN BELIEF:

My emotional responses are permanent and unchangeable; trying to change them will do no good because I will always respond to the same kind of situation in the same way.

Once we have developed a particular response to a certain set of circumstances, we are inclined to believe we will *always* respond that way. We think some occurrences will always make us angry, for instance, or others will always make us cry, but this is untrue. When we are angry, it is not because we have to be, but because we *want* to be. If we feel unhappy, it is not because unhappiness is unavoidable, but because we have *chosen* to feel that way.

COUNTER-BELIEF:

My emotional responses are a matter of choice.

We are not locked into any particular emotional response forever; we have a *choice* about how to react. It may not feel like we do because past conditioning makes our habitual choices seem natural. No matter how we have responded to certain kinds of situations in the past, we *can* choose to react in a totally opposite manner in the future. All it takes is our decision to do so. Having the *capacity* to experience various emotions does not mean we *must* experience them any more than owning a gun means we must fire it, or owning a piano means we must play it. Emotions are a choice we continue to make from moment to moment, and we are free to make a different choice whenever we wish.

*

*M*ISTAKEN BELIEF:

My negative emotions are caused by others' behavior toward me and by the unpleasant events that happen to me.

Our culture encourages us to believe emotional suffering is triggered by external causes, and it would be eliminated if people would be nicer to us and if circumstances would go our way for a while. To support this belief, we are trained to use conventions of speech which seem to prove it, phrases such as, "You made me cry," or, "You made me angry," or, "I didn't mean to hurt your feelings." Statements like these obscure the facts because they ignore the true cause of emotional problems. They simply attempt to shift the blame for originating them away from us and toward those persons or situations *appearing* to prompt them.

When we say to someone, "You make me absolutely furious," we imply he needs to change because he is making us feel so awful. Even if we *can* sometimes persuade others to accept the blame for our emotional problems, though, ultimately, the solution will prove unsatisfactory because it may remove the symptoms but not the cause.

If we try to get others to change so we can avoid emotional discomfort, we have misunderstood its point altogether. It is convenient to blame other persons for making us feel bad, but granting people so much power leaves us defenseless and vulnerable. It means we must live in the hope others will always be kind enough to look out for our feelings, even though experience has demonstrated they will not. Viewed objectively, trying to get others to change their behavior so we will stop reacting negatively is like hitting our head against a wall while begging the wall to stop hurting us.

It is not necessary to remodel the world and everyone in it to relieve our emotional pains because the source of the problem is much closer to home. In all our searching for relief from our emotional problems, we have neglected to try the only solution guaranteed to work every time: that of changing *ourselves* so we no longer respond the same way. *It is our response that causes our emotional pain, not persons or events.*

We have inflicted all this suffering on ourselves because we have failed to realize the truth:

Counter-belief:

Since my emotions are entirely under my control, I, and not others, am responsible for my emotional pain.

Our emotions originate *inside* us, beginning with what we think. Therefore, we are 100% responsible for them *ourselves*. Regardless of what others may do or what awful events may take place, the only way anything outside us can enter our mind is through our thoughts, and we have absolute control over them. Nothing that happens can cause us to experience *any* kind of emotion, *unless we willingly cooperate with it.*

So accustomed are we to blaming people and occurrences for our emotional problems, we may find it difficult to believe we cause them ourselves. After all, we consider ourselves rational, and rational people do not intentionally inflict pain on themselves. That is the point; the beliefs that cause us to experience emotional pain are *not* rational, and we inflict pain on ourselves without being aware *we* are the ones doing it.

If we think about it, we will realize it is impossible for anything outside us to cause us emotional suffering. If people and events actually have the power to affect *one* person's emotions, then they should affect *everyone's* emotions exactly the same way. If one person cries in response to another's sharp words, then we all should, and this is obviously not what happens. People and events may provide the *stimuli* to which we respond, but it is our *thoughts* about them and the physical responses those thoughts initiate that combine to create our distressing emotional feelings. Although we may believe we are acted upon by others, in fact, we act on our *thoughts* about them and then experience painful negative emotions *we cause ourselves*. If others appear to be able to influence our emotions, it is only because we have agreed to let them do so. The wonderful part is, we are free to withdraw our permission at any time.

DISADVANTAGES TO LETTING OUR EMOTIONS RULE US

We Lose Control Of Our Lives

A key element of self-esteem is feeling we are in control — not of the world or of other persons, but of ourselves. When we fail to understand *we* create our own emotional states, we lose that control, and with it, our self-respect. We behave like puppets, jerking and twisting about in response to others' moods and fancies. By allowing emotions to control *us*, we do not *act*, we *react*. Instead of feeling in control, we feel powerless, as though a force stronger than us is directing our lives. If we grant people and events in our lives the right to dictate our behavior, then we do not operate from *our* ideas of what is best; we let our environment tell us how to behave. When it does, it is not necessarily in ways which benefit us.

We Misinterpret Reality

If we permit harmful emotions to guide us, we will often behave irrationally because they distort our view of reality and prevent us from seeing circumstances as they are. With a mind clouded by emotion, our thinking is erratic, confused, and irrational; we are unable to concentrate; we tend to act first and think later. The more intense our emotional state, the more likely we are to behave foolishly and against our best interest. Considering the sometimes disastrous consequences of our actions, it is no wonder we think poorly of ourselves when we let our emotions, instead of our brain, control our behavior.

We Become More Prone To Illness

Our bodies, if we force them to absorb the shock of negative emotions over a long period of time, are likely to end up with ulcers, high blood pressure, premature aging, any number of stress-related diseases, and other physical disabilities, along with an immune system too weakened to fight them. On the other hand, if we cease bothering ourselves emotionally when life fails to conform to our ideas of how it should treat us, we will not only feel happier and more loving, we will discover an unsuspected reservoir of energy.

A NEW LOOK AT OUR EMOTIONS

Changing Habits of Emotion

To many of us, the idea that we can control our emotions is a new one. Trying to control them may feel strange and awkward to begin with because we are so in the habit of looking outside ourselves for their cause. Having to admit to ourselves that others actually have no emotional power over us is like throwing away a crutch we have leaned on for years. At first we will feel uncomfortable, but the longer we are without it, the stronger we grow. Finally, we are able to see it was not an aid but an encumbrance.

We Cease Trying to Control Others

It is difficult to admit we have only ourselves to blame for our emotional problems. Nevertheless, it is still the truth. It is no one else's responsibility to assure our emotional welfare; it is *our own*. This fact may be hard to accept, but there are positive aspects to it which more than compensate for any discomfort. Once we fully grasp that *each of us causes our own emotional pain,* others' actions can be a matter of complete indifference because we know *we* have control over the pain. When we stop expecting people to adjust their behavior to suit us, we can stop complaining when they fail to do so. Rather than letting external sources determine our moods, we can take charge ourselves and feel calm and happy, *no matter what others say or do, or what goes on in our lives.* By assuming the initiative, we take control and are at liberty to react as we choose — *not* as circumstances impel us.

We Stop Feeling Guilty

Yes, there is a price for accepting emotional control because we have to assume responsibility for causing our own emotional states. However, it is a small price to pay for freeing ourselves of a heavy burden of guilt. If we are responsible for *our* emotions, then others must be responsible for *theirs.* Unless we physically compel people or intentionally set out to provoke them, we have absolutely no reason to feel guilty when they respond negatively to our actions. This fact alone is enough to release many of us from a lifetime's accumulation of guilt.

EMOTIONAL CONTROL IS FOR EVERYONE

Emotional self-control is not a special ability granted to only a fortunate few; it is an option open to us all. We can permit others' actions to prompt our emotional states, or we can respond to the direction of our inner voice. However we choose, the fact remains: our emotional well-being rests in *our* hands and in no one else's. Until we accept that *we* cause our emotional problems, we will go on having them. If we continue to experience emotional pain, we do so by choice. Nature is infinitely patient, though, and each moment presents us with fresh opportunities to make better decisions. All of them, if we are perceptive enough to see them as such, are chances to select more wisely than we have done before.

*

INCREASING YOUR AWARENESS

1) Listed below are some sentences that imply our emotional problems are externally caused. On a sheet of paper, rewrite them to indicate you accept full responsibility for your emotions, rather than blaming them on someone or something else. For example, you would rephrase the sentence "You made me mad!" to "I chose to become angry about something you did," and so forth. Remember, how you feel is *your* responsibility.

> a. "You made me cry."
> b. "You hurt my feelings."
> c. "This weather is depressing."
> d. "I am so lonely."
> e. "I hate it when things go wrong."
> f. "I get furious when someone calls me names."
> g. "You really disappointed me."
> h. "You embarrassed me so badly."

Think of similar sentences you use, add them to the list, then rephrase them. Practice saying the rephrased sentences until you can do so comfortably.

2) Recall a recent situation in which you responded to another person's behavior with negative emotions. After giving the matter some thought, write how you could have responded if you had chosen to avoid becoming upset. Visualize the same situation occurring again, but in your visualization, react positively, or at least neutrally to the same stimulus to which you responded negatively before. Use new language or actions you believe would have helped you avoid a negative response. Repeat this exercise whenever you have problems remembering you are in charge of your emotions.

AFFIRMATIONS

I am the only one who can control my emotions.
I can replace unpleasant emotional responses with ones that support me.
I can choose new emotional responses whenever I wish.
Any emotion I experience is of my own choosing.
I create my own moods.
I refuse to make myself feel bad when things don't go as I wish.
I refuse to punish myself by experiencing painful emotions.
I don't have to accept the blame for others' emotions.
As soon as I change my thoughts, any emotional pain will go away.
My emotions are caused by me, rather than by others.
Others are responsible for their emotions, as I am for mine.
It is pointless to punish myself by feeling bad.
Since I control my thoughts, and my feelings are caused by what I think, I control my feelings.

* * *

8

The Past

MISUSING OUR MEMORY

As human beings, we have the unique ability to consciously recall memories with great clarity. We replay some of them so vividly they almost seem to be happening again. While we sometimes use this talent to good advantage, we abuse it by bringing the past into the present more often than we should. The problem, then, is not with this remarkable ability, but with how we use it. It would be one thing if the memories we recalled were happy ones, but we are not nearly so selective. We tend to focus our attention more on *unpleasant* recollections and, in remembering them, subject ourselves once again to their punishing emotional blows.

Making Ourselves Miserable

Unpleasant experiences are hardly uncommon; at one time or another, we all have them. Some are trivial, like being kept after school or being embarrassed in front of friends. Usually incidents like these have a negligible emotional impact, so they are usually soon forgotten. Other occurrences, however, have a more serious content, like a disastrously unhappy love affair, a serious accident, a life-threatening illness; or possibly undergoing something as deeply disturbing as rape, sexual abuse, the death of a loved one, or being forced to commit legalized murder in armed combat.

When events such as these happen, we may find them difficult to forget. Because we generate such intense feelings in response to them, our emotion-charged memories seem to take on a life of their own. With a morbid sort of fascination, we replay these painful recollections again and again in our minds. We remind ourselves of every detail, we feel the injury anew, and we re-experience the hurt and the emotional turmoil we felt, sometimes with even greater intensity than originally.

Negative Emotions Harm Our Self-Esteem

Although this kind of mental review may seem harmless, in fact, it is just the opposite. This is because distressing experiences like this have one thing in common: in all of them, *we cast ourselves in the role of victim.* When we react to an incident with intense negative energy, it is because we feel weak, helpless, and unable to defend or protect ourselves from someone or something we consider bigger and/or more powerful. The more often we remind ourselves of painful circumstances like these, the less we respect ourselves. Without exception, they add to our feelings of inadequacy by emphasizing our lack of power and control.

Although we may not be consciously aware, whenever we allow harmful emotions to dominate us, we forfeit our feeling of inner direction and permit ourselves to be controlled by people and events outside us. Each time we mentally review an unpleasant experience, we chip away a little more self-esteem. As we remind ourselves again and again of the fear, anger, sorrow, or humiliation we felt, we reaffirm our victim status and strengthen our belief that we are incapable, incompetent, or unlovable. The worse the picture we paint of ourselves, the less we feel we deserve anyone's love, *including our own.*

CHANGING OUR MINDS

The good news is that it is unnecessary to be troubled by unpleasant memories; we can eliminate their pain whenever we like. Obviously, we cannot go back and change past events, but it is not the events themselves that bother us — it is our *thoughts* about them, and we *can* change those.

OUR MISTAKEN BELIEFS ABOUT THE PAST

*M*ISTAKEN BELIEF:

Certain incidents are inherently disturbing. They affected me negatively and painfully because they would affect anyone that way.

We are guilty of assigning too much importance to disagreeable events from earlier in our lives. Besides this, we incorrectly believe they will continue to have a lasting, damaging effect on us. Are these occurrences truly as awful as we think they are, or do we give them more significance than they deserve?

If it were possible to get inside people's minds and experience their memories and emotions as intensely as our own, we would discover two things. First, *our disagreeable memories are far from unique; many people have had the same sort of events happen to them that we have.* Second, and more important, we would discover that *others' ideas of what constitutes an awful or horrible occurrence can be vastly different from our own.*

There are people who are horrified at the thought of having to speak in public. Others can imagine nothing worse than being trapped in the same room with a dog, a rat, or a snake. Experiences we might consider terrifying, others may think of as unimportant, or even as exciting or enjoyable. For instance, some persons would be shocked into paralysis if they had to jump or were pushed from an airplane flying at 5000 feet, even if they were equipped with a parachute they knew would function perfectly. Skydivers, on the other hand, actually appear to enjoy the sensation. The point is this: it is not the experience itself that makes us feel awful; *it is the way we think about it, how we perceive it.* No universal agreement exists about what does or does not constitute a terrible event; it is purely a matter of personal interpretation.

COUNTER-BELIEF:

No event is inherently painful or awful; it is only as painful or awful as I decide it is.

If particular situations from the past seem extremely disturbing, it is time to reconsider them, to try to see them differently than before. No matter what kind of experiences we may have had, or how distressing or awful they seemed when they happened, we are free to re-evaluate them whenever we choose and learn to see them in a less harmful way.

*

MISTAKEN BELIEF:

The pain of certain memories will be with me forever.

All of us have heard the saying, "Time heals all wounds." It would be more accurate to say we simply have less time to think about the old wounds as newer ones take their place. Unless we make a special effort to keep particular memories alive, even the most distressing are likely to lose their importance as it becomes necessary to devote our attention to memories more recently acquired.

There is a circus act which illustrates how we keep disturbing memories fresh in our minds. In it, a performer places a dinner plate on top of a pole. Then he spins the pole, which starts the plate spinning. This done, he stands the pole with the plate spinning on top of it on end, picks up another pole and another plate and repeats the process until he has five or six plates in motion. As the speed of the plates begins to slow, he runs from one pole to the next, giving each a few more spins to keep it going. If he doesn't, the plates stop spinning and fall to the ground.

This is remarkably similar to how we keep painful memories alive. Every time we recall something from the past and re-experience the emotions we previously associated with it, we add to its power and keep it active in our minds. The only reason our recollections seem so real is that we continue to "spin" them by giving them attention and fresh emotional reinforcement. The less we recall them, the fainter they grow.

COUNTER-BELIEF:

If I deliberately refuse to entertain painful memories and stop providing them with emotional fuel, they will lose their power to disturb me.

*

MISTAKEN BELIEF:

Certain periods in my life were extremely unhappy because only bad things happened to me.

Specific parts of our lives may stand out in our memories because we consider them times of great unhappiness. Life is rarely all good or all bad for anyone, though. Though there may appear to be more good than bad at times, or vice versa, generally people's lives are a mixture, of good *and* bad, happiness *and* unhappiness.

If this is true, however, why does thinking about certain times recall such painful feelings? It is because our predominant memories of a particular time determine our prevailing impression of it. If we have chosen to focus our attention on the negative occurrences of a period, we tend to think the entire period was unpleasant. If particular times seem more disagreeable than otherwise, it is not necessarily because they *were* but because we have been ignoring the happier parts and recalling only the unhappy ones.

To change our feelings about a particular time, we reverse the process by reviewing that period and focusing on only its *positive* aspects. These do not have to be events of great importance. They may be as simple as the friendliness of nurses when we were ill in a hospital, or others' thoughtfulness in response to a death in our family. If we look for positive aspects to almost *any* situation we have been involved in, we will find them. When we do, let us give our attention to them for awhile. By emphasizing the positive, we will cease identifying with the past's ugly souvenirs. Unless we are determined to make ourselves miserable, it is unwise to make an unfortunate event or condition the focal point of our life, no matter how devastating it once seemed.

COUNTER-BELIEF:

My feelings about any part of my life depend on which memories I choose to emphasize, rather than the actual events that occurred then. I can change the quality of my life by choosing to stress pleasant memories.

MISTAKEN BELIEF:

Past events, especially experiences that affected me strongly, will always influence my life and behavior.

Is it reasonable to blame our present behavior on unpleasant experiences from our past or to believe something that happened long ago still has the power to influence us negatively today? We cannot deny past events may still affect us, but whether their effect is good or bad depends entirely on our attitude. There is no doubt experience is an important teacher nor that distressing situations are sometimes the source of valuable lessons. But rather than letting go of these painful episodes once we have grasped their message, we tend to cling to them as tightly as we would a precious treasure and go on reliving them long after any educational value has been exhausted.

But is it particularly *sensible* to do this? Are the bitter memories we have so carefully stored away actually worth the effort it takes to remember them? Is there genuine benefit in recalling past problems? Will thinking about them improve anything, lessen our pain, or decrease our anguish? Can wallowing in old misery make us happier, more relaxed, easier to get along with, or a more pleasant person? Does it make us more successful, more generous, or more loving? Does it — *in any way* — add to the quality of our lives? Only those who are foolish or obstinate would answer anything but "no" to these questions.

True, we can use painful incidents from the past as excuses for our failures or as reasons to explain or justify inappropriate or self-defeating behavior we indulge in today. Using the past to explain away our present shortcomings does not help us in the long run; it just allows us to gain a little time, to postpone exchanging the role of a dependent child for the adult status which should, in fact, be ours.

Clearly, there is no advantage to building our lives on the wreckage of earlier problems or in poisoning our minds with toxic emotional residue. Nor is there any benefit in weighing ourselves down with the anchor of a painful past.

There are, though, plenty of good reasons why we should *not* burden ourselves with outdated mental debris. By looking at life through the eyes of the past, we restrict our growth; as long as we remain mired in bitter memories, we will stay where we are and go no farther. Holding on to old patterns of behavior keeps us from developing new behavior more suitable for the present. If we mistakenly blame the past for today's problems, we ignore our inherent strength, our flexibility, and our ability to adapt our actions to new circumstances. Even worse, refusing to let go of what has gone before means we will continue to view the world from a victim's perspective and to be victims, not just in our minds, but in our lives.

COUNTER-BELIEF:

If past events still influence me, it is not because they must, but because I choose to let them.

Except for what we can learn from it, the past is unimportant because *it no longer exists.* The only period of time with any value, and the only time for which we are truly responsible, is *right now*, this present moment. To the degree we direct our attention to the past, we make it unavailable for use in the here and now. Only by opening ourselves fully to the present can we effectively deal with it. And only by deliberately turning away from the past can we avoid being in a position where, instead of savoring the present moment to the fullest, we are, as Everett Shostrom put it, " still nibbling on the undigested memories of the past."

*

A STORY

Two monks were walking through a forest one afternoon on their way to a nearby monastery. Approaching a swiftly flowing stream, they saw a young woman weeping bitterly, standing on the grassy bank. "I was just starting across the stream," she said, "when the footbridge broke. I cannot swim and now I can't get home to my children. What shall I do?"

Taking pity on her, the older monk offered to carry her across the stream. The other monk looked at him sharply because the rules of their order prohibited physical contact with women. The woman, however, happily accepted the monk's offer, whereupon he picked her up and waded carefully across the wide stream. When he put her down on the other side, she gave him her grateful thanks and hurried into the forest toward her home and children.

As the monks continued their journey, the younger monk was unable to stop thinking about the other monk's actions. The more he thought about it, the angrier he became. With every step he took, he grew more enraged. Finally, after several miles, he could stand it no longer. "Brother," he accused, "you have acted in disobedience to your vows. You are a disgrace to our order. God will surely punish you." He went on in this manner for several minutes until finally, running out of accusations, he demanded to know if the older monk understood how seriously he had erred by carrying the woman across the stream. "Brother," the older monk replied quietly, "I set the woman down two hours ago. You are still carrying her."

*

INCREASING YOUR AWARENESS

1) Think of an irritating experience that happened to you a short while ago. Now sit back, close your eyes, and relax. Replay the incident, and as you do, be sure you remain comfortable and at ease. See yourself in the irritating situation you experienced, but review the scene objectively, as though it were happening to someone else. If you feel yourself starting to tense up, consciously relax. Keep going until you reach the end. If you felt any irritation when you replayed the incident, then repeat this process of objective observation until you do not. After a number of repetitions it will become so boring you will no longer feel like thinking about it.

When you first begin practicing this exercise, avoid using it for extremely painful memories. Until you can "defuse" moderately unpleasant past experiences, it is unwise to try a major overhaul. As usual, the best course is to proceed slowly but steadily.

2) Bringing paper and pencil with you, sit down where you won't be interrupted. Down the left-hand margin on the paper, write the numbers 1 through 20. Now think back to a day in the not-too-far-distant past when something disagreeable happened to you. As a result of your unhappy memories of the incident, you may recall the entire day as unhappy. So if you have predominantly painful memories about it, make a game of trying to recall as many pleasant aspects as possible, while ignoring the *unpleasant* ones. As you refresh your memory about the enjoyable aspects of the day, write them down. Here are some questions for starters:

1. Was the weather nice?
2. Did you eat anything you enjoyed?
3. Was anybody friendly to you?
4. Did anyone pay you a compliment?
5. Was there anything funny to laugh about?

6. Were you wearing something you liked?
7. Did you feel good physically?
8. Did you talk with anyone whose company gives you pleasure?
9. Did you hear any music you especially like?
10. Was anyone especially considerate or thoughtful?
11. Did anything unexpectedly nice happen?
12. Did anyone smile at you?
13. Did you watch any form of entertainment you liked?
14. Did you have plenty to eat and drink?
15. Were you hugged or touched by someone?
16. Did you read anything you liked?
17. Was your health good?
18. Did you make any enjoyable plans for the future?
19. Did you do anything particularly well?
20. Did you see or play with any animals you enjoy?

You can probably come up with other questions that are better, more effective, or more appropriate for you. As you may have gathered, the purpose of this exercise is to intentionally emphasize the positive aspects of situations we currently regard as predominantly negative. Identifying the pleasant memories helps us to get a more neutral and, consequently, more realistic view of the time.

AFFIRMATIONS

I let go of painful memories from my past.
I open myself to the present, accepting the good it brings me.
The past is over. I let go of it.
I free myself to live in the present.
*Since it is impossible to change the past, I accept its lessons
  and go on.*
I respond to the present, instead of the past.
I choose to stop dwelling on the pain of past injuries and hurts.

If I recall the past, I concentrate on only pleasant memories.
Events from the past affect me only if I choose to let them.
I expend my energy wisely by living fully in the present.

* * *

9

Making Mistakes

"It's only those who do nothing that make no mistakes, I suppose."
JOSEPH CONRAD

*M*ISTAKEN BELIEF:

I must always make correct decisions and avoid mistakes; if I do not, I am dumb or stupid.

Rather than showing ourselves mercy when we make a mess of things, we are critical, demanding, and unforgiving. We fail to grant ourselves the freedom to make mistakes. Errors in judgement we willingly overlook when made by others, assume massive proportions when we make them ourselves. We look back on our incorrect decisions, agonizingly wishing we had handled certain situations differently. Because we associate our feelings of self-worth with our ability to avoid mistakes, we guarantee ourselves a continual series of emotional ups and downs. Somehow we have arrived at the totally incorrect conclusion that we should never make mistakes. In fact, just the opposite is true.

COUNTER-BELIEF:

It is perfectly normal to make mistakes, even some pretty awful ones. My mistakes are no reflection on either my intelligence or my worth as a person.

THE FACTS ABOUT MISTAKES

Everyone makes mistakes. Making mistakes does not set us apart from the crowd; it puts us squarely in the middle. As every history book shows, we humans have *always* made mistakes, and there is no indication we will ever stop. If this is true, though, why do we not hear more about mistakes *others* make? First of all, we *do* hear about some of them, especially those made by famous people. We don't hear about a lot of others because our associates usually do not feel good enough about themselves to admit them. If we possessed the ability to read their minds, though, we would probably find them littered with the same kind of unproductive mental debris we have in ours: guilt, remorse, and regret for their mistakes.

Mistakes are unavoidable. Since we are fallible human beings, at times we cannot avoid making mistakes. We do not make them because we are stupid but because we lack information which would allow us to avoid them. As wonderful and versatile as is the human mind, it contains a limited number of facts on which to base our decisions. We don't truly *have* a choice, in the sense that we're aware of all *possible* options, because there is no way we ever can be. We consider the alternatives we know of during the time available, then choose the course of action which seems to promise the most positive outcome with the fewest drawbacks.

Consequently, the *only* reason we ever make unwise decisions is that we do not possess sufficient knowledge to make better ones.

Mistakes provide us with feedback. Mistakes are a healthy and valuable part of learning and are necessary to our growth as human beings. We *have to* make a certain number because that is the only way we can learn certain things. Instead of thinking poorly of ourselves for making them, we need to remember that every time we make a mistake we have found another thing that *doesn't* work and increased our chances of finding something that will. By generously allowing ourselves freedom to make mistakes, we improve our skills and increase our chances of success. While it is true experience is the best teacher, if we are to benefit from it, we must be willing students.

We make comparatively few mistakes. Sometimes we are so overwhelmed by our errors we fail to take into account the many correct decisions we *do* make. The process of living requires us to make thousands of decisions each day, many of which we are unaware of making. With so many opportunities for error, it is unreasonable to expect all our choices to be perfect. However, compared to the vast number of wise, life-enhancing decisions we *do* make each day, our mistakes are actually few.

We all make decisions we later regret. If we were able to predict the future with the accuracy we expect from ourselves, our skills would make us highly sought-after. When the coat we bought at full price is offered for half price the following week, we criticize ourselves as though we had prior knowledge of the price reduction but deliberately chose to ignore it. In fact, this sort of situation only emphasizes how easy it is to know how we should have handled a particular situation *after* it has occurred, when more desirable courses of action become apparent. Any Monday-morning quarterback can tell us how the game *should* have been played — once it is over. By then, of course, it is too late for the information to do us any good. What this clearly demonstrates is that, given enough knowledge, we will always make the best decision.

Our mistakes are not unique. We flatter ourselves by thinking our mistakes are both unique and worse than others', because, no matter what kind of mistakes we make, or how horrible they seem, they are not original; they have been made before, countless times by countless people and will probably continue to be made as long as the human race exists. Although the time, the details, and the circumstances may differ, when it comes to mistakes, there is nothing new under the sun.

We are wise to avoid punishing ourselves for mistakes. We may as well understand that we *will* make mistakes. While we are at it, let's be clear that complaining *to* ourselves *about* ourselves will improve nothing. Heaping blame and guilt on ourselves simply reinforces the idea that we make poor choices. This, in turn, makes us fearful and rather than making us more careful, increases chances we will make even *more* errors.

By the same token, we can avoid many mistakes simply by being less concerned about making them. If we do not insist on perfection from ourselves, we will feel less pressured and more relaxed, and consequently, will be less likely to make mistakes. Rather than agonizing over past errors, our time could be better spent considering how to eliminate the behavior which brought them about. Once we thoroughly grasp that all our actions need not be perfect, we will eliminate a substantial amount of stress and discomfort from our lives.

It is important to be tolerant of our mistakes. Our unwise choices or mistakes are never intentionally wrong; none of us goes to bed at night determined to make ourselves miserable the next day. Although we don't always know what is best to do, there is one thing we *can* be sure of: regardless of how matters turn out, we *always* make the wisest decision we can under the circumstances, given the knowledge we have — *at that time.* Another significant benefit to increasing our self-tolerance is the less blaming we are toward ourselves, the more compassionate and understanding we become toward others.

We Are always OK, even when we make mistakes. Behaving less than perfectly does not make us less than perfect human beings. There is no connection at all between our worth as a person and how many or what kind of mistakes we make. What we *do* is not the same as what we *are*. Just as we do not become good persons by avoiding mistakes, we do not become bad ones by making them. With or without mistakes, we are *always* OK.

It is fine to admit mistakes. Doing so is not a confession of inadequacy but an acknowledgement of our humanness and a testimony to the health of our self-esteem. If we believe we must always appear to be right, either in our eyes or anyone else's, we are trying to live up to an impractical ideal. We should be willing to acknowledge our errors, no matter how big or foolish they seem. We will only become error-free as we take our last breath. As long as we continue to make mistakes, it means we are still alive and learning.

Will we ever possess enough information to be *positive* we are making the right decision? No, and neither will anyone else. Try though we may, we will always be the fallible human beings we are now. We are not perfect, nor will we ever be. Making mistakes is not shameful; it is an inevitable and natural part of being human, as well as a means by which we develop and mature. Rather than condemning ourselves for making errors, we must learn to patiently accept them. The less we demand personal infallibility, the more comfortable we will be. The more willing we are to make mistakes, the easier we will find it to learn what they have to teach us. Having high self-esteem does not mean we won't *make* mistakes. It means only that having made them, we do not agonize over them or blame ourselves; we simply acknowledge their lessons and move on.

*

INCREASING YOUR AWARENESS

1) Think about a mistake you made recently. Using the following format, write the facts about your error.

    A) What was the mistake? Describe it.

    B) What were your thoughts leading up to it?

    C) Did it occur to you the outcome might be different than you anticipated?

    D) What were the negative results of your actions?

    E) Do you understand your part in making the mistake?

    F) Which of the following was the reason for the mistake?

        1. you were unaware of the consequences

        2. it was habitual behavior

        3. you forgot the results of similar situations in the past

        4. you were unaware of better alternatives

        5. you were afraid to change your customary behavior

    G) Has anyone you know ever done anything similar?

    H) How would you behave in the same kind of situation now, based on the information you gained from the experience?

Repeat this process whenever you make what you consider a serious mistake. As you do, you will become more forgiving toward yourself and cease blaming yourself for unavoidable errors.

2) Here is an exercise to provide you with a genuine understanding of how common mistakes are. At the top of a sheet of paper, write, "Everyone makes mistakes, including famous people." Underneath this, on the left side, write the name of a well-known person, either current or historical, followed by a

mistake he or she made. You might start with Columbus, who found America by mistake, or Napoleon, who made the mistake of fighting the Battle of Waterloo, or some past U.S. presidents who made serious errors, both in and out of office. List at least 20 famous people and a mistake each made.

Now title another sheet of paper, "Everybody makes mistakes, including people I know." Follow the same procedure as above, but list the names and mistakes of people with whom you are acquainted. This may be a little harder because we are sometimes inclined to overlook others' mistakes. Give yourself a little time for this exercise and list at least 20 in this group, too. A good time to practice this exercise is when you begin complaining about how terrible your mistakes are.

AFFIRMATIONS

I give myself the freedom to make as many mistakes as necessary.
I grant myself the freedom to be wrong.
I am always worthwhile, no matter how many mistakes I make.
I consider everything that happens to me a learning experience.
I use my mistakes as learning experiences.
I forgive myself for all my mistakes.
I am not my actions.
I was wrong, and I admit it.
I have a right to be wrong.
It is OK for me to be wrong.
I am worthwhile even when I do not live up to my expectations.
When I am uncertain what to do, I consider the consequences.
I learn from my mistakes without feeling guilty or blaming myself.
When I make decisions, I do so as wisely as I can.
I am not alone - everybody makes mistakes.
I am imperfect, and I accept my imperfections.
I am understanding, patient, and gentle with myself.

I am thoroughly worthwhile even when I make mistakes.
My mistakes contribute to my personal growth.
I forgive myself for not knowing the effect of my actions before I make them.

* * *

10

Guilt

"...no matter how horrible we have judged our past actions, *each day our life begins anew.*"
KEN KEYES, JR.

*M*ISTAKEN BELIEF:

I should feel guilty if I do something wrong.

"If only I'd...", "I wish I hadn't...", "Why did I...", "I should have..." These phrases, and numerous others like them, are all-too-familiar expressions of guilt. While we often accept human failings and imperfections in others, a nagging voice inside prevents us from extending the same forgiveness to ourselves. From infancy onward, we have been inundated with information about certain actions we must do if we are to escape penalty and others we must avoid doing at all cost. We have heard these from parents, friends, schools, churches, social organizations, and governments. Each has its own values, code of ethics, rules of conduct, or laws. If we act contrary to any of them, even if other persons do not find out and chastise us, we punish ourselves by feeling guilty.

THE ORIGIN, DEVELOPMENT, AND PURPOSE OF GUILT

What Is Guilt?

Guilt is not just one emotion. It is a combination of feelings we cause ourselves to experience to show disapproval of certain of our actions: anger, because we have behaved badly; shame, because we believe we have done something that is beneath us; and embarrassment, because of what others think or might think if they knew what we had done. To put it another way, guilt is the sincere wish we could undo something we have done or do something we have omitted doing, accompanied by feelings of self-loathing and disgust.

Guilt Is Unnatural

We enter this world with the capacity, but not the ability, to feel guilty. Although our primitive ancestors transmitted certain instinctive emotional responses to aid us in survival, guilt is not among them. None of us is born with a natural ability to feel this powerful, negative emotion. Guilt can be experienced only in regard to beliefs about right and wrong. If it were possible to feel it as newborns, that would mean we were born with an innate knowledge of right and wrong, which is clearly impossible. Only as we begin to learn about life are we taught to label some actions "bad" and others "good."

How We Learned to Feel Guilty

Parents teach their children to experience guilt in much the same way animals are taught to experience it by their trainers. A dog trainer, for instance, who wants her animals to avoid certain kinds of behavior, will reprimand them by saying something like, "Bad dog! Shame on you!", or similar phrases, when they do something she dislikes.

We humans learned the emotion in a similar manner. If we did something our parents disliked, they reproached us, telling us how awful we were for doing it and how ashamed we should feel for our actions. If we were too young to understand their words, then, like animals do, we sensed their displeasure from their facial expressions and tone of voice. Even if it was unclear just why our actions were so dreadful, our belief in our parents' superior wisdom was usually sufficient to convince us to accept their judgement of our actions and, consequently, to feel properly guilty and ashamed.

Why We Are Taught to Feel Guilty

Guilt is one of the most powerful and effective manipulative tools ever discovered. It is used extensively by those who believe, for one reason or another, they have a right to control our behavior. The easier others can make us feel guilty, the easier they can get us to behave as they wish. Those of us who can be encouraged to feel the most guilt are the most easily manipulated.

It is easy to understand why our parents used guilt as a teaching tool. When we were too young to grasp the consequences of our actions, simply explaining why we should or should not do a particular thing was not always sufficient to get us to alter our behavior; we needed a more easily understood incentive to guarantee our cooperation. By persuading us to associate guilt with behavior they disliked, they tried to insure we would always behave as they wished.

Although dogs can usually be trained to stay off furniture when their owners are present, it is often a different story when they are gone. There is a pet-training device that can be used to solve this problem. It is placed under a cushion on the pet's favorite piece of furniture. If the animal jumps onto it, its weight triggers a recording of the owner's voice, which reprimands his pet as though he were actually there. Similarly, if our guilt teachers trained us thoroughly enough when we were children, we probably still avoid certain acts they prohibited, even though as adults we are capable of making our own decisions about them. If we should give in to temptation and perform activities once forbidden to us, we may feel as guilty as we would if they were looking over our shoulder.

EVOKING THE GUILT RESPONSE

The Three Categories Of Guilt

1) **Guilt by hearsay.** We have been trained to experience guilt when we deviate from values we learned as children. We feel this sort of guilt when we do, or think about doing, certain actions others have told us are wrong. Often, there is no evidence to prove they are actually harmful and our own experience and observation have not indicated they are. All we know is *others* believed they were wrong, and by persuading us to feel guilty if we indulged in them, they passed their belief on to us.

Some actions that fall into this category do so as a result of beliefs which are little more than superstition. These include many actions we have been assured are bad or sinful. Usually, we learned about them from our parents, the clergy, or other well-meaning people who wanted to control our actions for what they believed was our own good. They used guilt to make us conform to principles, ethics, and morals which seemed appropriate to *them* but may not necessarily be so for us.

Little of what we believe to be wrong is wrong by our own determination. Others may have tried to keep us from doing certain things simply because we were acting in opposition to their desires. But if other people have performed these supposedly impermissible actions without ill effects, or if we have done so ourselves and not noticed anything terrible happening to us or others as a result, there is an excellent chance the people who trained us were wrong. Probably they were only passing along hearsay told to them. Regardless of their motivation, we have no reason to continue to feel guilty because of others' beliefs and preferences. If we do, we are just beating ourselves up because somebody told us to. If we have yet to observe evidence of the harmful or destructive nature of previously forbidden actions, we may wish to consider dropping our negative beliefs about them from our belief system.

2) **Guilt by accident.** We usually experience guilt when our actions have an unexpectedly undesirable effect. Although we may always act with the best of intentions, actions sometimes backfire and cause unexpectedly unpleasant results, as the following story illustrates.

A local church asked a friend of mine to perform as organist one Sunday while their regular organist was on vacation. In selecting music for the service, my friend inadvertently chose a hymn that a member of the congregation associated with her recently deceased husband. During the playing of the hymn, the widow, who was not yet over her husband's death, began sobbing and had to be escorted from the church. Even though it was impossible for my friend to have known how the song would affect the woman, he blamed himself for her grief and her emotional outburst. Despite being repeatedly assured it was not his fault, he felt guilty about it for weeks. He was so conditioned to feeling guilty that as far as he was concerned, the problem was not the woman's (who perhaps should have stayed home until she was fully recovered), nor the minister's (who might have asked to approve my friend's choice of music), it was *his* because he had picked that particular song.

If we feel guilty about this kind of situation, it is because we believe:

> a. we have the power to predict the future and know the effects of our actions before we perform them, and
> b. it is our responsibility to be aware of everyone's individual idiosyncrasies, pet peeves, personal sensitivities, and sore spots.

Unless we deliberately set out to produce unpleasant results, we have no reason to feel guilty about not anticipating others' responses. None of us is gifted enough to foresee all possible repercussions of our actions.

3) **Guilt by empathy.** We feel guilty when we have *knowingly* done something to another we would not want done to us. If there *were* a valid reason for feeling guilty, this would be it. But even this kind of guilt is irrational and illogical.

It is senseless to blame ourselves for behaving as we did at a certain time. If we had known then what we know now, we would have behaved differently than we did. Since we did not, it is foolish and self-defeating to speculate in this fashion. Every decision we make is the best and only one we *can* make at the time, based on our background, knowledge, and awareness. It might be appropriate to feel guilty if doing so would alter our past actions, but this is clearly impossible. What has happened, has happened. Punishing ourselves with guilt will help neither us nor anyone we have harmed. What we can do, though, is imagine the discomfort or pain we would feel if we were in the same position in which we have put others. By doing this, we have done the best thing we can to prevent ourselves from committing the same kind of act again.

If we feel guilty about something for which we believe we should apologize or make restitution, then by all means let us make amends, unless our attempts to repair the damage might make the situation worse. Once we have acknowledged our mistake, understood why our actions were harmful, and determined not to repeat them, what more can we do? Standing knee-deep in guilt and punishing ourselves by dwelling on our mistakes just makes us more miserable and lowers our self-esteem further. This kind of behavior is more likely to cause problems than it is to prevent them, and it will not improve the situation in the slightest.

COUNTER-BELIEF:

Guilt is an inappropriate, harmful, and unnecessary response to any action, no matter how serious the consequences.

WHY GUILT IS HARMFUL

Does feeling guilty ever help anyone? Not even slightly. Guilt has no redeeming qualities. It makes a situation worse, not better. It is harmful, mentally, emotionally, and physically. It is an unproductive dead end, a waste of valuable time and energy that could be far better spent on something worthwhile. No activity is more useless and injurious than condemning ourselves because we cannot change the past.

Guilt Affects Our Self-Esteem Negatively

Guilt and low self-esteem go hand in hand. Guilt is self-inflicted emotional punishment based on illogical feelings of unworthiness. It makes us feel we are lower than low, scum of the earth, despicable, awful, indecent, contaminated.

When we feel guilty, we automatically dislike ourselves. It is hard not to when we are disgusted with our behavior. How else *can* we feel when guilty memories keep popping up to remind us how awful we are? When we feel guilty about a situation, the powerful negative emotions we feel "freezes" it in our memory, providing us with a vivid mental movie of our shameful errors. Trying to make ourselves feel better, we replay them, hoping to discover some redeeming aspects to make it seem less awful than we believe it is. Unfortunately, this usually has just the opposite effect, and we end up feeling worse about ourselves, instead of better.

A Rational Approach to Guilt

We can learn from mistakes only if we stop condemning ourselves for making them. Guilt, rather than helping us remain open to learn from past errors, constricts our thinking and closes our minds to further growth in that particular area. By causing us to constantly associate painful feelings with our mistakes in judgement, guilt *increases*, rather than diminishes, the likelihood of repeating them. On the other hand, if we refuse to let guilt trouble our minds, feedback from our experiences will usually show us how to avoid the same kind of error in the future.

It is unnecessary to continually refer to past errors to learn from them. What we must do is recall the lesson and forget the situation where it originated. In the interest of peace of mind, we must always remember, *all the guilt in the world will not help us go back and change even **one** thing in the past.* When we are tempted to give in to damaging feelings of guilt, we need to remind ourselves that we — *like everyone else* — are imperfect human beings with human frailties and limitations. Nothing we have done, no matter how awful we or anyone else believes it is, is so bad we should not forgive ourselves for having done it. This is what we must learn to do, because if we are not able to forgive ourselves, it makes little difference who does.

*

INCREASING YOUR AWARENESS

1) Think about something you've recently done that makes you feel guilty. Using the following format, list the facts about the situation.

A) Describe what happened.

B) What were your thoughts leading up to the incident?

C) Did you intentionally set out to harm anyone?

D) Did it occur to you ahead of time what you were going to do might have unpleasant repercussions?

E) What was your reason for doing as you did?

   1. you were unaware your behavior might cause problems

   2. you misjudged the seriousness of your actions

   3. you behaved as you customarily did

G) Has anyone you know ever done anything similar?

H) Whose voice do you hear telling you that you should be ashamed for what you've done?

I) Did your actions result in problems for another, or did they cause no apparent harm?

J) If you were faced with an identical situation now, would you repeat the same behavior, knowing what you now know?

Perhaps the question of greatest significance is, "Would you repeat your behavior, knowing what you do now?" If you would not, then, unless there are inescapable consequences as a result of it, you have paid for your mistake as much as you need to.

Repeat this process whenever you do anything you feel guilty about. As you do, you will become more understanding and forgiving toward yourself and cease blaming yourself for unavoidable errors.

AFFIRMATIONS

I forgive myself for being imperfect.

I am not my behavior. My worth as a person is unrelated to my actions.

I have nothing to feel guilty about. I always do what I believe is best at the time.

I let go of unwise decisions from my past.

I accept the consequences of my past actions, but I refuse to punish myself by feeling guilty.

I accept my actions without feeling wrong because of them.

I feel guilty about nothing, because given my present awareness, I always do the only thing I can.

Feeling guilty will not change the past.

I release any negative feelings about my past behavior.

Nothing I have done, no matter how awful it seems, lessens my worth or value as a person.

I recognize my past mistakes as unwise decisions, rather than reasons for guilt.

✳ ✳ ✳

11

Changing Others

"Nothing so needs reforming as other people's habits."
MARK TWAIN

"We may consider that the other fellow behaves like a fool, but we must learn to give each and every individual the right to be a fool in his own fashion."
LEWIS F. PRESNALL

PEOPLE'S BEHAVIOR OFTEN
LEAVES SOMETHING TO BE DESIRED

At times, others' behavior is a great trial to us. And the closer a relationship, the greater its potential for irritation. Why do we find others' actions so provoking? With some people it is their habits, mannerisms, way of speaking, viewpoint or general attitude toward life. We find others exasperating because they are discourteous, rude, unkind, abusive, or they fail to take our needs, wants, and feelings into consideration as much as we think they should. Whether their faults are major or minor, when others' behavior bothers us, we try to persuade them to act differently, even if we have to exert a great deal of pressure to get them to do so.

Convincing Others to Change

We are endlessly creative in our attempts to eliminate others' undesirable behavior. Sometimes we simply point out their errors, naively assuming they will be happy to make immediate adjustments once we make them aware a problem exists. We may express our wishes as a reasonable request or a matter of principle, explaining how much their behavior bothers us and how much happier we would be if only they would change it. If that is insufficient, then we are willing to repeat our plea indefinitely, each time adding more emotional weight to it. If this fails, we try disapproving glances, sullen unpleasantness, childish tantrums, and in especially difficult cases, full-blown rages. In fact, we have a whole portfolio of manipulative techniques from which we can draw to encourage others to become as we want them; we correct, remind, urge, cajole, plead, beg, prod, nag, insult, wheedle, whine, threaten, coerce, or intimidate, to name just a few. What is truly amazing about this procedure is not the lengths to which we will go to persuade others to change but that we behave so obnoxiously ourselves, with the intention of getting *others* to change *their* objectionable behavior!

PROBLEMS WITH CHANGING OTHERS

We Are Seldom Successful

Trying to convince people to change can be extremely frustrating. Our efforts often go unappreciated, or we encounter a lot of hostility. Worst of all, we're usually unsuccessful; rarely do the changes we hope for take place. If we look at our track record, we will find losses far outnumber wins. Although at times it may appear we have won, these victories are often only temporary; just when we think we have eliminated a particular problem, up it pops again in a new and different disguise. If we do manage to persuade someone to change, it is usually only at the expense of bitterness and hard feelings between us and those we have so ambitiously tried to reform.

Sometimes our attempts to get others to change backfire and have just the opposite effect of what we intended. This happens because the more we comment on or emphasize a certain aspect of someone's behavior, either good *or* bad, the more likely it is to increase. Ironically, all the time we imagine we are drawing closer and closer to victory, our efforts are actually reinforcing the same behavior we are so anxious to erase.

If, despite our conspicuous lack of success, we go on trying to change people, it is clear we have not yet understood why we have failed: the project we have taken on is not just difficult, it is practically impossible. Regardless of how much energy we are willing to put into it, the results of our labors can be summed up in just a few words — futile, pointless, disappointing, and discouraging.

Why Our Efforts Fail

Like so many other problems, our difficulties in persuading others to adjust their behavior to better meet our expectations occur because of beliefs that are at odds with reality. Small wonder then that our attempts so seldom meet with success.

INCORRECT BELIEFS ABOUT CHANGING OTHERS

*M*ISTAKEN BELIEF:

Other persons should behave according to my standards of behavior.

We take for granted that our intelligence, ideas of right and wrong, ethics, morals, sense of justice, inherent goodness, sense of propriety, or some other part of our mental or psychological makeup is superior to others. To us, *our* way is the right way and their way is *wrong*. If we did not think this, we would not be so insensitive or hypocritical as to presume we were in a position to judge them. The egocentric naivete with which we so blithely assume we are morally or intellectually superior to others and our demand that others adopt *our* beliefs and *our* ways, would be amusing if only it did not cause so much harm to the lives of innocent people.

Do we have any proof, besides our own opinion, that our ideas are better or more accurate than others? Or evidence proving beyond a doubt that our ways, our beliefs, or our actions are preferable to theirs? We do not. Inevitably, we are disappointed when we try to impose our standards, values, and expectations on others because they have their own. While we may be able to convince *ourselves* we know what is best for others, we often encounter stubborn opposition when we try to convince *them*. As far as they are concerned, *we* are the ones looking through the wrong end of the telescope; their standards of behavior are right, and ours are wrong! All the while we have been waiting for them to conform to *our* ideas of right and wrong, they have been waiting for us to adapt to *theirs*!

COUNTER-BELIEF:

Other people's standards of behavior are rightfully different from mine.

*

MISTAKEN BELIEF:

People should be willing to change because I want them to.

This belief ignores the fundamental fact that other people are just like us; they're the way they are because they believe there is an advantage to being that way, even if only to avoid the discomfort of change. Unless we can present them with an exceptionally convincing case for the behavior modification we propose, chances are that is exactly how they will stay.

It is not that people are unable to change; they can, and they will, but only when they believe it is clearly to their advantage and that by doing so they will improve matters for themselves one way or another. Rarely does anyone consider our wanting them to change sufficient reason to do so.

COUNTER-BELIEF:

If I expect others to alter some aspect of their behavior at my request, I must be prepared to offer them an incentive they value.

*

MISTAKEN BELIEF:

My behavior does not irritate others as much as theirs bothers me.

If we believe this, it is only because we are so preoccupied with ourselves that we fail to pay attention to those around us. True, we should always accept ourselves completely, faults and all, but we must realize not everyone will see eye-to-eye with us on this matter. If the truth were known, others may be even more irritated by our behavior than we are by theirs. If they seem less eager to change us than we are to change them, it is probably not that our behavior is superior to theirs, just that they are more tolerant than we are.

*C*OUNTER-BELIEF:

Although I am free to disapprove of others' actions, I must not overlook that they may just as thoroughly disapprove of <u>mine</u>.

*

*M*ISTAKEN BELIEF:

If there is something I dislike about others' behavior, it is their responsibility to change it.

The reasons we offer people to support our requests for them to change *seem* legitimate enough: we tell them it's for their own good, or it's the right way to do things, or we only want what is best for them, and so forth. Our real purposes, though, are considerably less unselfish.

Our efforts to persuade others they are in the wrong are just a smoke-screen behind which we hide to avoid the central issue. The question we should address is not how can we make our efforts to change others more effective, but why do we expect them to change in the first place? *Why, when our relationships are not as we wish, do we automatically assume change is the other person's responsibility?* For an extremely practical reason, for if we can convince others it is *their* obligation to change, then *we* are relieved of the burdensome and unwelcome need to change ourselves. By labeling *their* behavior "wrong" and *our* behavior "right," we try to put them in a position where they feel they must alter their behavior to correct the situation.

But do we have the *right* to expect or even ask people to change their behavior, so we can avoid changing ours? Of course not. It is not anyone else's obligation to make us feel good; it is our own.

COUNTER-BELIEF:

If I am unhappy with others' behavior, unless they are infringing on my legitimate rights, it is up to me to change, not them.

What is there to prevent *us* from changing ourselves? Absolutely nothing. It is no more difficult for us to alter our behavior than it is for anyone else. Furthermore, the only person over whom we exercise complete control, and consequently, the only person we *can* change, is ourselves.

If we are unhappy with what is going on in our lives, then we need to look inward to ourselves, not outward to others. If we are bothered by another's behavior, rather than relying on him to change, we can solve the problem quite neatly by simply choosing *not* to become irritated. As long as we believe others cause our problems, we will continue trying to change them. This will never work, though, because the solution to our problems lies in *ourselves*, not in them! Until we accept that *we,* need to change, not others, we will waste precious time trying to cure the wrong disease.

WE ALL HAVE THE
RIGHT TO BE DIFFERENT

Tolerance is in short supply for a disturbingly large number of us, both as individuals and as a society. We are inclined to confuse our personal preferences with moral imperatives; we forget that people are not bad people simply because they do things we dislike. Calling them nasty names or describing them as "bad" doesn't *make* them bad any more than calling a pond an ocean will add a drop more water to what is already there. Although we may disapprove of others' actions when they behave contrary to our wishes, they are merely exercising their prerogative to do, be, and think as they choose. Unless their behavior is physically harmful, intentionally disruptive, or infringes on our or others' rights, what people do is no one's business but their own.

As difficult as it may be for us to grasp, people have the right to be as they are, *whether or not we like it.* We must permit them to have their own opinions and to see things their own way. We must grant them the liberty to be as *they* wish, even if that does not coincide with *our* wishes.

People have the right to live as *they* see fit, rather than according to our expectations. By letting them follow their own blueprint for life, we are not doing them any special favors; we are simply giving them the same thing *we* want — the freedom to be ourselves. We are not required to like what others do or agree with their values, but it is essential to our emotional health that we learn to accept them as the reality they are.

BENEFITS OF LETTING
PEOPLE REMAIN AS THEY ARE

Both our and others' lives will be far more pleasant once we learn to accept their differences instead of complaining about them. Dwelling on people's imperfections, whether imaginary or real, only prevents us from appreciating their positive aspects. By understanding others rightfully object to modifying themselves merely to make the world more pleasant for us, we will ultimately avoid a lot of unhappiness and hurt feelings. Once we cease trying to manipulate others' behavior and drop our preconceptions about how they *should* behave, we will cease being disappointed by their actions.

We, too, will benefit from a changed attitude on our part because when we are intolerant, we do not limit our intolerance exclusively to others. If we continually criticize other persons, our judgmental attitude spills over into our feelings about ourselves, and as a result, our self-esteem grows progressively worse. On the other hand, by adopting a more accepting attitude, by trying to increase our understanding, and by steadily refusing to judge or condemn others, we become more compassionate and less blaming — not just toward them, but toward ourselves as well. As a further bonus, once we have fully accepted that others' behavior is their responsibility instead of ours, we will find we have a great deal more time available to spend on improving our own.

*

A STORY

Many years ago, in a faraway land, lived an unhappy king. In many respects he was well satisfied with his life. He lived in a beautiful palace, his subjects were devoted to him, he had servants to carry out his every wish, and altogether, he led quite a comfortable life. Despite the luxury surrounding him, the king wasn't satisfied. What he wanted to do more than anything else was to walk through his kingdom and visit with his subjects. Since his own life was so pleasant he wanted to find out what he could do to make their lives happier. He hadn't been able to gratify his wish because the land throughout his kingdom was extremely rocky. So much so, that whenever he walked on it, the soles of his feet (which were *exceedingly* tender to begin with) got so badly cut and bruised it was impossible for him to walk without great pain.

One day the king had an idea; he sent out word for all the wise men in the kingdom to come to the palace. Surely, with their combined wisdom, they could find the answer to his problem. When all had assembled, the king explained the situation and asked how long it would take them to reach a solution. After conferring with the others, the oldest wise man said, "Give us three days, your majesty, and we will have your answer."

"So be it," said the king and had them shown to the council chambers so they might work undisturbed.

The three days passed quickly for the wise men. No matter how many ideas they came up with, none seemed even slightly practical. Finally, on the evening of the third day, they sent a messenger to the king. They had a solution, they announced, and would present it the following morning.

Eagerly, the king entered the throne room the next morning. He looked expectantly at the wise men. As before, the oldest spoke: "Your majesty, the solution to your problem is to slaughter all the cows in the kingdom, and once their hides have been cured, have them placed on the ground to cover the rocks and protect your feet."

"How long will this take?" inquired the king, hoping it could be done in several months. "Ten years, your majesty," the wise man replied.

"Ten years!" thundered the king. "I might be dead by then. If this is the best answer you can come up with, perhaps I should start with *your* skins." (He wouldn't have, of course, because despite his royal temper, he was an extremely *fair* king.)

Just then the court jester, who had crept in quietly while the wise man was addressing the king, spoke from the corner of the throne room, "If it please your majesty, would it not be simpler to kill just *one* cow, and after curing the hide, have it cut and sewn to cover just your feet, instead of the entire kingdom?"

So it was that the first shoes were invented and the king learned it was sometimes easier to change yourself just a little bit than try to change the entire world.

*

INCREASING YOUR AWARENESS

1) On a sheet of paper, write the name of someone you associate with or see on a frequent basis, who does something you dislike. (It is best to start practicing this exercise with something that just affects you mildly; behavior with a highly negative effect should be worked on only after some practice.) Next, write what bothers you about the person. Now imagine being with that person and seeing her or him do the particular thing that irritates you. Instead of becoming annoyed, say to yourself something like, "I feel completely neutral about John's habit of making noise when he eats. John does what is right for him, not for me. Life is different for John than for me. I can't expect him to understand my feelings about his behavior any better than I understand his. I accept that I cannot control his behavior."

If you practice this exercise on a continuing basis, using various friends or associates as the basis, you will become less and less judgmental of people, *including yourself*. The idea is to bring you to the point where you fully accept that the only life you have a right to try to change is your own.

2) Draw a line down the center of a sheet of paper. On the left side list the names of people whose behavior troubles you and next to their names the particular actions you find annoying. In the other column, opposite each name, write either A) behavior of yours that same person has criticized, or if there is none, B) behavior of yours you know has been commented on negatively by others.

Take care not to use your "questionable" behavior as a reason to reproach and condemn yourself. This exercise is intended to make clear that we, too, engage in objectionable behavior. The next time you're ready to criticize someone, remember — others may be as eager for you to change as you are for them to.

3) Set aside 15 minutes each day to be non-judgmental. Make an agreement with yourself to refrain from criticizing, complaining, condemning, or making value judgements about anything or anyone during this period. If you find 15 minutes too long a time

at first, split it up into 5 minute increments. When you reach the point where you are successful doing this for 15 minutes, add another 15 minutes. Keep doing this till you develop the habit of being non-judgmental.

4) Think of someone you dislike and list why you dislike them. Since everyone is as they are for a reason, try to imagine what kind of experience might have caused this person to develop the character traits you dislike. Would the same kind of experience cause you to behave as he or she does? If not, what would make you behave similarly? Repeat this exercise until you run out of people or behaviors you dislike.

AFFIRMATIONS

I hold others blameless, knowing they do the best they can at any time.

I accept the right of others to see truth in their own way.

I allow others the freedom to live life as they choose, regardless of how I think it should be lived.

Since all of us do the best we can, I feel empathy and compassion for others.

I accept that all of us are doing the best can in light of our present awareness.

I accept others without judging either them or their behavior.

Everyone does his or her best, given the limitations of their understanding.

I realize others are not their appearance or their behavior.

I do not blame others for my problems or mistakes.

I accept that I am unable to control people or circumstances.

I have no right to attempt to control others' actions.

* * *

12

Competition

"...we act competitively because we are taught to do so, because everyone around us does so, because it never occurs to us not to do so, and because success in our culture seems to demand that we do so."
ALFIE KOHN

*M*ISTAKEN BELIEF:

My worth can be measured by my success in competitive situations.

Being a winner, being able to surpass others in competitive situations, is highly valued in our society. Because we grant winning such significance, competitions of all kinds play an important role in our lives. Before we are even old enough to understand the mechanics of competition, we have already become unwitting rivals with other toddlers, because our parents are eager to determine who among us is the cutest, the biggest, the smartest, who smiles the most, or began walking or talking the soonest. Once we enter school, we are expected to be involved in sports and other competitive activities.

Our competitive efforts are not limited strictly to formally organized contests. We compete for the highest grades in the classroom, the highest score on the athletic field, and the highest wages in the workplace. Our home, our place of employment, and our social circle all serve as arenas for our talents, giving us the opportunity to prove — if only to ourselves — we are the most loving parent, the friendliest or most helpful person in the office, or the smartest and best-dressed of our acquaintances.

Unwilling to relinquish the chance to compete even during our leisure time, we engage in recreational competition with games such as bowling, tennis, and golf. Social gatherings find us immersed in card games, board games, and word games. If we are unable to compete or to win ourselves, we identify with specific athletes or teams, immerse ourselves in their contests, rejoice in their victories, and bask in their reflected glory.

Our desire to be recognized as winners is exploited thoroughly as opportunities to compete increase daily: Cutest Baby, Sexiest Grandparent, King of Hearts, Queen of the Prom, Miss Galaxy, Mr. Personality, and so on to the point of boredom. Practically every quality, characteristic, attribute, talent, skill, or ability, which can be measured or rated in some manner, has become the basis for a contest.

Since competition permeates every level of our existence, it is small wonder we grow up thinking of it as an inescapable fact of life. So accustomed are we to competing that to many of us, existence would seem pointless if we were unable to gauge our progress by measuring it against others'. So caught up are we in the business of comparing ourselves with one another, that an unbiased observer might justifiably wonder if *any* area of our lives has escaped the relentlessly prodding finger of competition.

MYTHS ABOUT COMPETITION

A number of reasons have been given to explain why we compete, ideas aggressive people have put forward to justify their ambitious behavior. These popular, but erroneous, claims tend to surround competition with an aura of artificial respectability by arguing it is natural to compete and that competition works to our benefit.

Is Competition Natural?

The theory has been advanced that "human nature" causes us to compete, that competitiveness is an inborn characteristic of our species, so competition among us is inevitable. If this were true, though, members of *every* culture would engage in competitive activities. Anthropological evidence indicates there are societies in which competition is a totally foreign concept. Besides, for a trait to be considered human nature it must be or have been, possessed by every human being who has lived on this planet, from the beginning of the species up to the present. The facts simply do not bear this out. If competition feels natural, it is only because from infancy onward we have been immersed in the notion that competition is not only unavoidable but is actually *desirable*.

Does Competition Bring Out the Best in Us?

Some persons believe competition brings out the best in people, inspiring us to strive harder and enabling us to achieve results superior to those achieved in non-competitive settings. An examination of the facts proves otherwise. Rather than bringing out the best in us, competition is dehumanizing, causing us to see fellow-competitors less as *people* than as objects, obstacles to be overcome on our way to the top.

Competition narrows our field of vision and limits our choices. If our main purpose for taking part in competitive activities is winning rather than the pleasure of the activity itself, our fear of failure makes us limit our endeavors to only those we feel confident we might win. Rather than encouraging us to do or to be our best, it only urges us to be better than someone else.

Competition does not inspire us to strive harder. Instead, it distracts us from what should be our main objective — doing the best job we can. When we compete, we are not free to give our full attention to the job at hand; we must continually turn away from what we are doing to compare our progress with others'. In competition, we do not seek accomplishment and improvement for their own sake, but for the boost they give our ego.

Rather than producing superior results, competition traps us in sterile conformity. Since competitors working to achieve the same goal must follow the same rules, the more they work to surpass each other, the more alike they become. Far from encouraging us to explore new territory, this imitative attitude restricts our view, making us oblivious to anything outside the confining course we have set for ourselves. Rather than encouraging us to be innovative and create new forms, competition forces us to fit ourselves into those that already exist.

Does Competition Help Build Self-Confidence?

Advocates of competition stress its importance in building self-confidence, stating it develops a feeling of competence in us and elevates our self-esteem. Unfortunately, rather than causing us to think better of ourselves, competition is likely to do just the opposite. Anyone who has been forced to compete — which in our culture means *all* of us — has experienced the shame and self-doubt that accompany losing. This is inevitable because built into every competitive conflict is the potential for embarrassment, for being revealed as a loser, for being proved inferior, sometimes publicly, *for the majority of the participants.* By its nature, competition requires *nearly all* competitors to lose *nearly all* the time. The actual danger to our self-esteem is that we will come to equate success in competition with our worth as a person. Then, faced with a series of losses, we begin to internalize failure and to think of ourselves not only as *losing* but as *losers*, judging ourselves inferior because we failed to win.

Even the self-confidence we supposedly gain as a winner is short-lived because ultimately, winning adds to our insecurity. True, for a brief time we live in the clouds, thrilled with our success and intoxicated by the taste of victory. Once the initial elation is gone, however, doubts begin to crop up. How could they not, because there is no such thing as a "permanent" victory.

Having once beaten others, we must *continue* trying to beat them. If we are to stay at the top, we cannot rest. Instead, we must intensify our efforts, all the while knowing one day *we* will be standing on the sidelines watching another receive the trophy so recently ours. If we do gain the title "winner," we may be sure it is only on loan; at this very moment there are others working to surpass us, only to be surpassed, in turn, themselves.

WHY WE COMPETE

What is behind our urge to compete? Our enthusiasm may be partially explained by financial considerations, by large cash awards or valuable prizes sometimes offered to winners. In fact, comparatively few competitive situations offer a financial incentive. So if not for money, why *do* we compete? We do so because we lack self-esteem and because we think competition is a means of proving to ourselves and to others we have personal value.

We Compete to Gain Others' Recognition

We take part in competitive activities because we desire others' recognition. Engaging in competition is merely a bid for approval on a massive scale. The more impressive the victory, we believe, the greater the approval. Winning means we will receive others' acclaim, their applause, and their acknowledgement of our superiority. It means for a time at least, we will stand out from the crowd and demonstrate for all to see that we are not just an undistinguished nobody but someone special. By attaining the status of champion we gain others' attention, and being noticed by others, we believe, is to *be* someone. Our goal is to prove to everyone what unique and valuable persons we are.

We Compete to Gain Our Own Approval

We compete, not because we *have* faith in ourselves, but because we *lack* it. Fueled by a belief in our personal inadequacy, our aggressive drive to prove our worth compels us to seek supremacy in any way we can. We see winning contests as proof of our worth, confirmation of our value. If we compete and win, we gain others' recognition, and by doing so, increase our feelings of self-worth. In other words, we want others' approval so we can use it as a springboard from which to launch feelings of self-acceptance. Our ultimate goal is to firmly convince ourselves we are better than we believe we are. This, we hope, will quiet the nagging voice inside us which continually reminds us that, on a fundamental level, we are no good.

*C*OUNTER-BELIEF:

My value as a human being is entirely unrelated to how I rate or compare with others, either in or out of competitive situations.

We Believe Being a Winner Adds to Our Value

We are inclined to think those who win are superior, not just in the area in which they have demonstrated their ability, but superior *in general.* Because we place excessive value on winning, we tend to think less of ourselves if we fail in competitive situations, as though winners are somehow better than losers. But winning makes us no more valuable than losing, and neither has the slightest bearing on our worth as persons.

WHY COMPETITION IS SO DEADLY

Contrary to popular belief, competition makes losers of us *all,* regardless of our official status at game's end. To compete, we must compare, and comparing ourselves with others has a negative rather than a positive effect. That our culture values competition so highly is not proof of its desirability, only of our individual and collective insecurity.

There is no question about competition's inherent harmfulness. It is a wasteful process. For me to get what *I* want, or "win," someone else must *not* get what she wants, or "lose." In working to achieve *our* goal, we must do so in such a way as to prevent others from reaching *theirs*. In other words, competition allows us to gain only by making others lose. And any activity structured to make one person feel good at the expense of making everyone else feel bad can be considered only *damaging and destructive*.

Competing Makes Us Dependent

Competition, by its nature, leads to degrading dependence. When we compete, we set others above us, using them as standards or guides by which to measure and rate ourselves. By adjusting our actions to copy theirs, we let ourselves to be directed *externally*, not *internally* as we should be.

Trying to gain self-esteem by comparing others unfavorably with ourselves doesn't work because it means we depend on them to give us a sense of self-worth. Relying on others' failures to make us feel worthwhile *weakens* our self-esteem, instead of reinforcing it. By intentionally competing, we brand ourselves not as winners, but as insecure, second-class individuals who must triumph over others to gain a feeling of personal value.

LIFE WITHOUT COMPETITION

Life itself is not competitive, but there are many competitive people who make it appear that way. We do not *need* to compete, and it is not *desirable* to compete. If we are content with ourselves, we will opt *not* to compete; we have no need to prove our worth to anyone, including ourselves. Rather than competing, our goal should be to develop as individuals, to become the best we can, regardless of how well or how poorly anyone else is doing.

Contrary to popular belief, removing competition from our lives will not encourage us to diminish our efforts but to increase them. Even without the pressure of competition we will still try to do our best, not because it is important to outperform others, but because using our abilities to the utmost gives us the pleasure of personal satisfaction. As far as the quality of our work is concerned, there is a vast and significant difference between actions generated by a desire to outdo others and those inspired by a desire to do well.

We should consider life not a race, but a leisurely journey, where each of us is proceeding at his own pace, rather than running to keep up with others. As Alfie Kohn puts it in *No Contest*, "...the real alternative to being number one is not being number two but being psychologically free enough to dispense with rankings altogether."

AFFIRMATIONS

Since we are all different, comparisons are useless.
I am a unique individual with unique strengths and weaknesses.
Winning or losing has no connection with individual worth.
It is impossible to prove my worth with my actions or achievements.
I do not let fear of failure or defeat concern me.
My worth as a person is unrelated to how well I do anything.
It is unnecessary for me to compete.
Competition is neither necessary nor desirable.
I do not become a better person if I win or a worse one if I lose.
Using my skills, abilities, and talents to their fullest extent gives me personal satisfaction.

* * *

13

Perfectionism

"...the desire for perfection is the worst disease that ever afflicted the human mind."
RALPH WALDO EMERSON

"There is no perfection or certainty in the world and to expect to find it is irrational."
GERALD KRANZLER

M ISTAKEN BELIEF:

It is important everything I do is done as perfectly as possible.

THE GENESIS OF PERFECTIONISM

Perfectionists Are Made, Not Born

Some parents make unrealistic demands on their children. Forgetting their own childhoods and children's inherent limitations, they judge their young by adult standards instead of by criteria appropriate for their children's age. They fail to realize children do not have the coordination, the understanding, or the sophistication to deal with a situation as quickly or as competently as an adult.

Even with the best of intentions, parents like these are demanding taskmasters, hard to please and rarely satisfied.

Regardless of what their children do or how well they do it, they expect them to try a little harder, work a little longer, do a little better. They dangle the ideal of perfection in front of their offspring like a carrot before a donkey, and furnish their children with adult examples by which to measure their childish progress.

Praise from these parents is rarely wholehearted: it is always tempered by contrasting how well their children *did* with how well they *could* have done. This, they believe, gives their children an incentive to do better next time. When young persons are unable to live up to their parents' unrealistic expectations, their parents rarely miss the opportunity to tell them how disappointed they are. To further emphasize their displeasure, perfectionistic parents often withdraw their love and approval from their children when they are dissatisfied with them. This leads their offspring to the conclusion that love and approval are not only conditional, but are dependent on standards to which they can seldom, if ever, measure up.

From a Child's-Eye View

When we were children, our parents were the most important people in the world to us, and we desperately wanted to please them. Since we were too young to realize *they* were at fault for asking too much of us, we concluded *we* were at fault because we were unable to meet their demands.

Over a period of time we came to accept their negative judgements of our abilities as accurate. We began to think of ourselves as never good enough, as always a little short of the mark. As a result of hearing the message "not good enough" repeated time after time, we internalized it; not only did we apply it to what we did, *but to ourselves as well.* Thus we began our career as a perfectionist and started the downhill slide to low self-esteem.

Although our original critics may no longer be with us, and may even be dead, their words have become a part of us. Based on memories of our imagined imperfections, we have created an internal critic, and we now criticize ourselves; the need to avoid mistakes and be perfect, which was once someone else's need, has become one we incorrectly believe is our own.

PORTRAIT OF A PERFECTIONIST

What does it mean to be a perfectionist? It means no matter how much effort we put into a task or how well we do it, we are rarely satisfied it is good enough; we still see ways to improve on it. Or to put it another way, because we persist in the delusion that perfection is attainable, we habitually set unrealistic, unachievable goals.

As perfectionists, we believe perfection is just around the corner. Just one more improvement, we think, just one little change, and then everything will be just right. "Oops!" we say, "How did I miss *that*? Well, as soon as I get *that* fixed and make two or three other changes, it actually *will* be perfect." Of course, as soon as those changes are made, we notice several *more* items that need to be changed, and so it goes.

SYMPTOMS OF PERFECTIONISM

When we become caught in the tangles of perfectionism, rarely is it limited to just one aspect of our existence; like a contagious disease, perfectionism spreads its infection throughout our entire system until we are overcome by it.

We Waste Time on Unimportant Details

When we believe perfection is a desirable and achievable goal, we waste a lot of time on unimportant details. We cross every 't' and dot every 'i' on projects of little significance. We become bogged down with trivial details and spend large amounts of time on relatively brief and simple tasks. We re-do work we have already re-done, although no one except ourselves will ever see it. Insisting on perfection in everything, we have difficulty establishing priorities. We find it hard to make decisions because we have come to mistrust our judgement as well as our abilities. To us, there is no such thing as "good enough"; it's always "just a little bit more." From our perfectionistic viewpoint, the journey is never over, the task never done, the project never completed. No matter how many people assure us we have already done well enough, we believe they say that only because their standards are lower than our own.

Instead of having attainable goals, we search for ideal solutions. We believe there is a perfect answer to every problem, and if we work on it long enough and hard enough, we will surely find it. So we go on correcting, changing, rearranging, and improving, endlessly chasing perfection like the pot of gold at the end of the rainbow.

We Insist on Being Right

As perfectionists, our feelings of wrongness often show themselves as a desperate need to be right. We take delight in pointing out others' mistakes. By doing so we try to put ourselves above them, so we will we feel less bad about ourselves. We may go to ridiculous lengths to prove we are right. We look for misspelled words (if we are good spellers), errors in etiquette (if we are sure *our* manners are flawless), lapses in morals (according to *our* standards, of course) or anything else that will make us appear to be superior persons with every right to point out others' flaws.

THE PAIN OF PERFECTIONISM

Being a Perfectionist Is No Fun

As perfectionists, we are seldom satisfied with ourselves as we are, so we constantly work at becoming better. We believe the more perfect we appear, the more we will be loved and accepted. The less fault people can find with us, we think, the less criticism we will receive and, consequently, the less reason we will have to dislike ourselves. We don't think of ourselves as perfectionists, of course, merely as people with extremely high standards.

We are overly concerned with our appearance, behavior, attitude, and anything else about us that is less perfect than we believe it should be. Since we judge our worth by how perfect we are, we *never* like ourselves well enough. Instead of valuing ourselves for being as we are, we strive for an artificial sense of value by trying to live up to unreasonable ideals imposed on us when we were small.

We severely restrict ourselves by demanding perfection. Since we shudder at the idea of being less than perfect, we limit ourselves to tasks we are positive we will do well, carefully avoiding any endeavor that might expose our lack of perfection to others or ourselves. Failing to grasp that sometimes just *doing* is more important than *doing well*, we turn away from pleasurable activities at which we may not excel.

The perfectionist's mind is a fertile breeding ground for emotional problems. By setting impossibly high standards we guarantee ourselves unhappiness. We inflict pain on ourselves for failing to achieve the impossible. We feel angry because hardly anything is as perfect as we want it to be. We feel guilty because we are certain our work is not good enough. We feel frustrated and exasperated by what we consider our imperfections, and we blame ourselves for them. Trying in vain to perfect our entire life, we feel hopeless, then depressed. Finally, a numbing despondency overwhelms us once we realize we will *never* be perfect.

How Perfectionism Sabotages Our Self-Esteem

Since perfection is rarely attainable, our inability to achieve the unachievable often causes us to be hounded by feelings of failure and inadequacy. We believe imperfection clings to us like a bad odor. Despite the show we put on for others, inside ourselves we believe we are not up to the mark, that we have a long way to go before we can be as good as we believe we must be. Because we equate our ability to be perfect and do everything perfectly with our worth as a person, we feel chronically unworthy because we can never seem to *be* enough or *do* enough. How can we possibly think well of ourselves, surrounded as we always are by evidence of our imperfection?

THE TRUTH ABOUT PERFECTIONISTS

Strange as it may sound, perfection is *not* the actual goal of the perfectionist, just the means to an end; our *real* goal is to gain the unconditional love and acceptance we failed to receive from our parents when we were small. We developed an obsession with perfection by equating our ability to please our parents with our worth as a person. As perfectionists, we are trapped in the corridors of the past, still searching for the approval we never received as a child. We do not crave perfection because it is desirable in itself but because of the feelings of "rightness" and "worthiness" we associate with it.

*C*OUNTER-BELIEF:

Perfection, or the lack of it, has nothing to do with my worth as a person. Striving for perfection is unnecessary and self-defeating most of the time.

Perfection Exists Only in the Mind

There is no point in taking perfection seriously because it does not exist. It is a fantasy, a self-defined ideal, an abstraction which exists only in people's minds. We live in an imperfect world, surrounded by imperfect circumstances and imperfect people. As history amply demonstrates, we human beings have always been imperfect. We look less than perfect, conduct ourselves less than perfectly, and because we *are* human beings, will never *be* perfect. Being imperfect is not only (perfectly) acceptable, it is inevitable!

How perfect *is* perfect, anyway? Almost every project can be improved on indefinitely in one way or another. The secret is in learning when to stop. There is no harm in trying to improve on our previous performance, but we must decide ahead of time at what point it will be "good enough." Every task has a degree of perfection appropriate to it; there is no need to apply the same amount of exactness to mowing a lawn as we would to cutting a diamond or handling dangerous explosives. Perfectionistic thinking is only a habit we've acquired that we can break by setting realistic cut-off points for everything we do.

Freeing Ourselves From Perfectionism

By imagining a relationship between our ability to achieve perfection and our value as a person, we needlessly diminish our self-esteem. The truth, of course, is our worth as a person is independent of *anything*, including how well or how poorly we do things. We are no less valuable for leaving work unfinished than we are for completing it with fanatical precision. And the voices which ceaselessly urge us on to perfection? They, like our concept of perfection, are not ours, merely some we borrowed from others long ago.

Our wholeness and human worth are existing facts, not qualities linked to our ability to put on a perfect performance. Intrinsic value is not a reward we can earn with a lifetime of endlessly perfecting ourselves; it is our birthright. Our ambition should not be to *do* everything perfectly but to understand we do not *have* to and to realize that perfection, rather than being a desirable goal, is one of the biggest barriers to a loving and uncritical acceptance of ourselves.

*

INCREASING YOUR AWARENESS

1) When you were a child, who were the persons who criticized your work by saying it wasn't good enough? As you identify them, write each name on a piece of paper. After the name, write some

things they said to you. If you are unable to come up with any phrases, then follow this process in reverse; first think of what *you* say to yourself when you are displeased with the job you have done, and then match it up with the name of the demanding person who said it to you in your childhood. Once you have identified your critics, you will be better prepared to talk back to them.

2) Select a task from some you'll be doing today or tomorrow. Decide right *now* just how detailed it must be. Establish a cut-off point *now* at which you will say, "I'm done." Make it a habit to set realistic cut-off points, and you will be happier and more productive.

AFFIRMATIONS

Being imperfect is perfectly acceptable.
I am worthwhile regardless of how imperfectly I do things.
I can quit when I've done things well enough, even if they're not perfect.
I stop working on tasks when they are done as well as they need to be.
I avoid becoming involved in unnecessary details.
I set reasonable and realistic standards for myself.
It is OK to be less than perfect.
There is no such thing as perfection.
How well I do anything is unrelated to my worth as a person.
I realize my desire for perfection is an ineffective coping mechanism from the past.
I accept and think highly of myself even when I do less than perfectly.
Striving for perfection will not make me more lovable or worthwhile.

* * *

14

Manipulation

"Manipulation plays on our weaknesses, touching our deepest fears and our strongest wishes, drawing its strength from our selfish desires. ...those who are skilled at manipulation may stir up strong emotions, leading us into actions which do not serve our best interests."
TARTHANG TULKU

*M*ISTAKEN BELIEF:

It is inconsiderate not to do what my friends and family ask me to do for them.

Too often we find ourselves doing things for people, not because we want to, but because there seems no way to get out of it. We put up with unpleasant relatives; we play chauffeur; we do favors involving great personal sacrifice or inconvenience on our part; we act nicely toward people we don't particularly care for; we pick up after others; we don't perform certain actions only because someone else believes we shouldn't; we perform other actions because someone else believes we should, and we go to ridiculous lengths to avoid hurting someone's feelings, to name just a few.

Even as we perform these pleasureless activities, we wonder, *"Why am I doing this?"* Intuitively, we know something is wrong, but we are unable to put our finger on it. Worst of all, though we sometimes desperately want to avoid being mixed up in these disagreeable situations, we feel powerless because we don't know how to refuse. Predictably, and with good cause, we feel victimized, so we respond with irritation, anger, and resentment. It is no wonder. Although we may not consciously realize it, we sense that control of our lives has somehow slipped from our hands into those of others.

Why, if we dislike such situations so intensely, do we permit ourselves to be drawn into them? Invariably, it is because we have been pressured to do so by others. They have persuaded us it is our duty to do certain things we have no desire to do, or to put it another way, we have been *manipulated.*

WHAT IS MANIPULATION?

Manipulation is speaking to and/or acting toward other persons with the intention of getting them to respond in a specific way but without making them aware of our intentions.

How Manipulation Works

Manipulators try to get inside our minds, so to speak, to discover our motivations and analyze our reactions. Once they have obtained a certain understanding of how we think, they employ that knowledge to their advantage, inducing a little guilt here, a little fear there, and drawing the responses they want from us by playing on our weaknesses as skillfully as a master musician does on his instrument.

If an acquaintance knows we usually become angry when a certain subject is mentioned, and he brings it up intending for us to become angry, he is a manipulator. When a woman who knows we like to be thought of as generous mentions an expensive gift she has received, hoping we will buy her something even more expensive to maintain our self-image, she is a manipulator. Parents who try to get their children to improve their grades by comparing them with better students are manipulators, just as their children are when they try to persuade their parents to buy them something because "everybody else has one."

Nowhere is manipulation more prevalent than in the advertising industry. Successful ad writers persuade us to buy products we would never consider getting if they did not first convince us we must have them. Using the manipulator's familiar tricks, they coax us to purchase by encouraging us to feel guilty or by implying there is something wrong with us.

We like to think we are independent thinkers, people capable of making up our own minds and choosing our own course of action. But if we are easily manipulated, there is a distinct possibility much of what we do is done, not because *we* want to do it, but because *others* have convinced us we should.

MOTIVES FOR MANIPULATION

The manipulator's goal is to persuade us to do something he thinks should be done that he believes we don't particularly want to do. Since manipulators are self-centered, that usually means something to benefit them personally — *in one way or another*. Despite their similarity of purpose, reasons for manipulation vary from one person to another. Usually, though, they resort to manipulation because one or more of the statements below are true.

> • *They are afraid to ask us directly because we might refuse.* Some persons think so little of themselves they believe we have a poor opinion of them, too, so they are concerned we will simply ignore their requests. Having no *real* bargaining power, they try to create some artificially.

• *They have little regard for the rights and feelings of others.* Frequently, manipulators have little concern for anyone besides themselves. They believe what they want us to do is more important than whatever we might decide to do on our own.

• *They are trying to gain power.* Understandably, manipulators often feel weak, insecure, and powerless. They sometimes gain a temporary feeling of strength and authority if they can control our actions.

• *They are unable or unwilling to do what they want us to do.* Some persons lack the skills and abilities to get what they want for themselves, so they are forced to rely on others. Rather than bargaining honestly, though, they try to trick us into helping them.

• *They are convinced certain things are due them because of their relationship with us.* Family members often irrationally think other family members owe them, merely because they are related. They use the fact of relationship to excuse their selfish, arrogant behavior.

Some manipulators engage in what might be termed "benevolent manipulation." People like this feel justified deceiving us because they consider their motives thoroughly praiseworthy.

• *They believe their morals or notions of right and wrong are superior to ours.* This conceited and egotistical belief encourages people to attempt to guide our actions to reflect their ideas of what is right, instead of our own.

• *They believe they are acting in our best interests.* Some people honestly, but incorrectly, believe they know what's best for us better than we do. Their attempts to manipulate us imply we're too ignorant or stupid to know this ourselves.

• *They believe the end justifies the means.* Some manipulators consider their goals so worthwhile they will unashamedly trample on the rights of anyone who stands between them and their objectives.

Although "benevolent" manipulators are not selfish in the sense they benefit directly from their efforts, they are nonetheless self-centered, self-serving, and self-righteous, because they believe they have the right to impose their wills on us. Regardless of how lofty they imagine their goals to be, their actions are no less damaging than those of manipulation for less "noble" purposes.

THE MANIPULATOR'S TOOLS

How do manipulators convince us to do what they want, especially if we don't want to? Effective manipulators prompt a feeling of obligation in us or convince us it is advisable to do what they ask or suggest. Since painful emotions are ideal for this, they are manipulators' strongest tools. Because there are so many, they have a whole toolbox from which to choose.

Guilt

Guilt is one of the most useful and versatile manipulative tools, which explains its great popularity. By implying we have done something we shouldn't have or have omitted doing something we should have, manipulators try to make us feel guilty and often succeed. It is unnecessary to have actually *done* something they consider wrong; they may criticize us for even thinking about doing it or for situations we had no part in and over which we exercised no control. Although the sentiment may have been phrased differently, nearly all of us were asked as children; "Don't you feel guilty leaving food on your plate when there are people who are starving?", as though cleaning our plate could somehow improve the situation for those who were going to bed hungry each night.

Being so universal in its application, guilt appears in a variety of manipulative disguises, some of which are listed here.

> *Hurt feelings.* Although we are not responsible for others' emotions, nearly all of us have been brought up to believe we are. So when someone tells us they will be badly hurt if we behave differently than they want us to, we usually do as they ask to avoid the guilt we would otherwise feel. If we have already done something that displeased them, they try to manipulate us into being less "thoughtless" in the future, by trying to impress on us how badly we hurt them by doing it.

> *Lack of consideration.* Some salespersons are masters at inducing guilt. They use it as a lever to ease us into a position where we believe we must buy whatever they are selling. The life insurance saleswoman who paints a nightmare picture of what could happen to our family if we were not heavily insured is an expert at provoking guilt. So is the tire salesman who tells us we are negligent to let our family ride in a car with less than the best (and incidentally, the highest priced) tires.

> *The test of love.* Some people try to manipulate us by implying we don't love them enough, or even at all, if we neglect to do as they ask. They demand we prove our love by doing whatever they request of us, as though it were possible for anyone to demonstrate the extent of her feelings in such a fashion. The irony of this is that anyone who asks us to show *our* love in this manner, clearly does not love *us*. When one person loves another, he does not insist she obey him like a faithful dog.

Those who demand we do view us less as fellow human beings than as their property.

Poor little me. Some manipulators approach their intended victims passively, acting helpless, indecisive, and clinging. Instead of spending their time learning to take care of themselves, they use it to convince us they are so weak they can scarcely lift a finger without our help. Usually they appear so pathetic that if we fail to help them, we feel heartily ashamed and load ourselves down with enough guilt to sink a battleship.

Great expectations. People sometimes try to influence our behavior by telling us exactly what they expect of us. By doing so, they make it clear we have two choices: we can either live up to their expectations and make them happy or fail to meet their criteria and disappoint them. In either case, they point out that the state of their emotions depends on us, and heaven help us if we let them down.

Approval or disapproval

People who know we value their approval may threaten to withhold it if we do not do as they wish. In some cases the manipulator is frank about what he wants and states the options, giving us the opportunity to choose. Despite its apparent openness, this approach is still manipulative; those who use it are pretty confident we will choose not to sacrifice their approval or they would not try this technique in the first place.

Some individuals use a positive variation on this theme, promising to like or love us if we do as they wish. This kind of offer makes it sound as though love is a prize given for meritorious or distinguished service. It is safe to say the "love" we receive for pleasing someone in this manner is rarely worth the trouble we go through to get it, no matter how little effort is involved.

These potent manipulative strategies are based on approval and disapproval.

> *Anger.* Being the object of someone's anger or extreme disapproval can be terrifying. Once people discover they can intimidate us by becoming angry, or by acting as if they were, they will use this emotion against us whenever it suits their purpose. However, as long as we are certain it will not lead to physical violence, this kind of anger need not concern us. If someone wants us to behave in a certain way, and all he is willing to offer us in exchange is withholding his anger, we are definitely getting nothing for something if we accept his deal. If others choose to expend their emotional energy so extravagantly, it is courteous of us to allow them the freedom to be as angry as they like.
>
> *Other-directedness.* This popular technique works as follows: the manipulator brings up an action we are planning to take and then urges us to reconsider because of how negatively she thinks people (especially herself) will view it. If she appears to be losing ground, she may attempt to support her position by bringing in an outside authority whose opinion is impossible to verify, like God or deceased relatives ("If your mother could only hear you").
>
> *Implying a deficiency.* If someone wants us to perform a particular action or behave in a specific way, he threatens to call us unflattering names, like "coward," "sissy," or something equally uninventive, if we don't. This schoolyard approach is effective only if we consider the other person's opinion of value and believe he will think highly of us if we do what he asks. More likely, though, he will think

less of us because we were so easily manipulated. Once we are able to see through his attempts to manipulate us, we will realize his evaluation of us is of little importance.

Flattery. This form of manipulation should be the easiest to see through, but because we generally have poor opinions of ourselves, it seldom is. If someone is willing to hand out compliments by the bucketful, we soak up every word she says and hope for more. Flattery makes us feel good about ourselves temporarily, and for that reason, we enjoy it. It is helpful to bear in mind that people who offer us gratuitous compliments typically have ulterior motives, and flattery is their way of getting us to rise to the bait. In the long run we usually find their praise is not worth the price we eventually pay for it.

Unfavorable comparison. To use this technique, the manipulator mentions someone who is superior to us in a certain regard and then pressures us to change our behavior by asking why we are not more like that person. Because of its ease and simplicity, this method is a favorite of parents who want to bring their children into line. As parents soon find out, there is a distinct disadvantage to using this technique. Most children quickly learn to apply it to their parents, comparing them with other parents who give their children bigger allowances, let them stay out later, are less strict, and so forth.

Although manipulative approaches based on guilt and approval are undeniably common, those grounded in fear, desire, and stubbornness are sometimes used, too.

Fear of consequences

Persons employing this technique use threats to add extra persuasiveness to their demands: if we do (or don't do) a certain thing, they tell us, we will be sorry later. Of course, if there are actual or potential hazards connected with a particular course of action, and someone is warning us of them, his attempt to caution us is not manipulative. Many times, though, the warnings we receive are empty ones, intended only to persuade us to behave as others wish.

Creating desire

To produce the results she wants, the manipulator points out how good we will feel or paints a picture of how rosy our future will be if we buy the product or service she sells. Typical remarks from this kind of manipulator are, "Think how much better you'll feel if you..." and "It will do you good to..." and "Wouldn't you be happier if..." Few people are as genuinely concerned about our welfare as this manipulator tries to make us believe *she* is.

Paradoxical intention

This is a reverse approach to manipulation, and it can only be used on us if we tend to be disagreeable and contrary. If we do, all the manipulator has to do is suggest we do just the opposite of what he actually wants us to do. Then if we behave true to form, we will do what he wants, rather than what he suggested.

MANIPULATION UNLIMITED

Considering the manipulative methods we've discussed, it is obvious some people will go to great lengths to control our actions. Given the seemingly limitless creativity of human beings, manipulation can appear in almost any guise and in almost any kind of situation. Effective manipulators are aware we probably will not be interested in doing what they want without some kind of incentive. Consequently, they are willing to engage in elaborate deceptions to persuade us to do as they wish. To avoid being caught in their traps, we must remember:

Counter-Belief:

Unless I have intentionally indebted myself to others, I am under no obligation to assume responsibilities or perform duties simply because they believe I should.

Unless we are involved in an employer/employee relationship or have agreed on an arrangement for compensation, we can say "no" when others ask us to do things. While it is one thing to honor an obligation we have knowingly incurred, it is definitely another to feel compelled to satisfy obligations only because *others* have decided we should.

Manipulation's Harmful Effects

It does not serve us to believe others will give as much importance to our needs as their own because they rarely do; we cannot rely on them to do what is best for *us* because their primary objective is to do what is best for *them*. To the manipulator, there is no question whose welfare is of greatest importance; ours is always secondary to her own.

Manipulation is dehumanizing. Manipulators don't see us as fellow human beings with rights of our own. They think of us as something to be controlled, somebody to get something from, an object which can be moved about like a piece on a chess board to best satisfy their needs and desires. Because they treat us like an object, we begin to feel like one. Whenever we are manipulated, we lose the control of our life so essential to self-esteem, both in fact and in feeling.

Why We Allow Ourselves to Be Manipulated

Why do we permit others to manipulate us? *First,* unless we see through the manipulators' deceptions, we fail to realize we have no responsibility to carry out their demands. *Second,* we do not want to run the risk of offending others; we want their approval, and we are afraid to say "no" because they might not like us any more. *Third,* it is likely manipulation feels natural to us; it is so commonly employed we probably use it on others and notice nothing strange about them using it on us. *Finally,* if we do realize we are being manipulated and protest, we usually receive the same reasons to comply we received as children. Because they are so familiar to us, it is habitual not to challenge them.

AVOIDING MANIPULATION

How can we escape the manipulator's clutches?

> • We need to become thoroughly familiar with the manipulator's techniques. The better acquainted we are with them, the easier they will be to avoid. If, despite our efforts, we find we have been manipulated into doing something we would rather not, then we figure out how it happened and how to avoid it in the future.

> •We must cease manipulative behavior ourselves. To escape being caught up in others' unreasonable demands, we need to stop making the same kind of demands ourselves. When we face a problem, we can solve it by manipulating the *circumstances* surrounding it, *not other people.* Once we have eliminated manipulation from our behavior, it will be much easier to dodge others' attempts to enslave us; rather than considering them legitimate requests with which we must comply, we will recognize them as the poor courses of action they are.

We do not try to change the manipulators themselves because that would involve manipulative behavior on our part. Instead, we change our response to their efforts and, by doing so, make it clear they are wasted on us.

• We must learn to say "no" and mean it. There are people who would like us to adjust our behavior to make life more convenient or pleasant for them. When we stop buying into their attempts to manipulate us, they will tell us we are selfish, self-centered, unreasonable, inconsiderate, and a whole lot of other words that signify we are not behaving as they want us to. This is to be expected. Those who complain the loudest and raise the strongest objections to our new attitude will be those who have most to lose by our declaration of freedom.

It is easy to understand why they are reluctant to loosen their hold on us; doing so means they will have to learn to stand by themselves or find another person to lean on. If we want to stop being their victim, we must be willing to risk their disapproval.

Another point to bear in mind: years of dealing with manipulators has given us the false idea that we must provide people with some kind of justification if we want to avoid doing what they want us to. This is a complete fallacy. *We are not required to provide explanations, reasons, or excuses for not wanting to do something. It is enough that we do not want to.* **Period.**

Our Responsibility

Nothing is wrong with doing favors for others — as long as we do them voluntarily and not because we have been pressured. Also, we have no reason to consider ourselves manipulated if we willingly perform services for others, even if they have tried to manipulate us into doing them. Our basic responsibility, though, is not toward others; it is to take good care of ourselves and avoid causing others harm in the process. This does not mean we should ignore our responsibilities to those who have a legitimate claim on us, but neither does it mean we must accept others' ideas of what is, or is not, our obligation.

If we want to enjoy others' company more and have relationships that are mutually comfortable, rewarding, and free of pretense, then avoiding manipulation from any perspective, whether as victim or perpetrator, should be our goal.

*

INCREASING YOUR AWARENESS

1) Divide a sheet of paper into two columns. In the left column, write something someone has said or done to get you to do things you didn't want to do. Opposite this, write a response you could have made that would have allowed you to maintain control of the situation. Continue this until you run out of situations.

To understand how to complete the next step, suppose an acquaintance said to you, "If you don't lend me fifty dollars, I'm not going to be able to pay my rent. You don't want to be responsible for my being thrown out of my apartment, do you?" Having been asked for loans by this person on numerous occasions, you knew she continually lived outside her means, and it was difficult getting her to repay loans. Consequently, you don't want to lend her money.

Previously, her pressuring you and the feelings of guilt she's encouraged you to feel have made you give in. Since people like this know all the answers to the standard objections you might make, using them is usually a waste of time. Now, however, you're going to prepare your strategy in advance, so you can maintain control in similar situations. What is your best bet in this kind of situation? You don't want to lie; you want to be factual, so you can speak with conviction. Your strategy: you reply, "I don't have any money to lend you." This is not a lie but a fact. If you do not want to lend money, then you have no money to lend, and that's a fact. You are not saying you don't have any money, which might be untrue, only that you have none to lend. To complete the process, repeat the statement until you can say it with certainty.

Follow this procedure for every item on your list. First, repeat what was said or done to you; second, prepare an honest response that will let you avoid doing it, and third, say firmly (out loud, or just in your mind) exactly what you will say in the future to escape this particular predicament. With some types of manipulation, it is helpful to simply rephrase what the other has said and begin the sentence with, "You think..." to indicate it's only the other person's opinion. Repeat each of your responses several times until you feel comfortable with them and can say them with conviction. Practice until this no longer feels like strange behavior.

2) Using the same list compiled in the exercise above, recreate the situation as vividly as you can in your mind. Imagine the other person saying or doing what he did then. Visualize yourself responding by replying firmly that you prefer not to do what is being asked of you.

Continued rehearsal of this behavior will make you feel comfortable with your new set of responses. This will prepare you for real-life situations where others may try to convince you to do things you don't wish to. After a period of time, your responses will become automatic, and you will become immune to others' attempts to control you.

AFFIRMATIONS

I do not permit anyone to persuade me to act against my better judgement.

I am under no obligation to do things simply because others think I should.

I do not allow others to use my emotions against me.

If others' approval depends on my doing what they wish, it is not worth the price.

When people try to make me feel guilty, it is because they want something from me.

I am free to say "no" when others make unreasonable demands of me.

When I do what people ask, I do it because I wish.

Whenever I am reluctant to do something others ask of me, I should ask myself why.

I do not let others make me feel guilty when I decide not to do what they ask.

I feel great knowing I do not allow myself to be manipulated.

* * *

15

Verbal Traps

Certain misleading phrases, expressions, and questions are the manipulator's stock in trade. We will refer to them as *verbal traps* because they seem to mean one thing but usually mean something entirely different. With a few exceptions, these patterns of speech don't merely distort the manipulator's intentions; they conceal them. Verbal traps differ from ordinary conversation in that they are spoken with the purpose of making others feel obligated or indebted to the manipulator. If he can get us off balance, so to speak, and convince us we owe him something, we will be more compliant and willing to cooperate than we would be otherwise.

Few of these verbal traps will seem new. It is likely we are well acquainted with them all, either because they have often been used on us or because we have misguidedly employed these patterns of speech ourselves from time to time. It is important to recognize them for what they are and become aware of how they work if we want to avoid being caught in others' verbal traps.

OTHER-DIRECTEDNESS

"What will people say if you do that?"
"What will people think?"

Obviously, it is impossible to answer these rhetorical questions. That is OK, though, because the person asking them doesn't want us to anyway. What she *does* want is for us to be so horrified that others might disapprove of us that we avoid pursuing what she considers a poor course of action. Because the manipulator is afraid her own opinion does not carry enough weight, she often brings out the heavy artillery of others' disapproval to support her arguments, hoping it will so intimidate us we will behave as she wishes.

Sadly, some people genuinely believe others' attitudes toward them are so important they will adjust their behavior to avoid the least hint of disapproval. Because they do, they are trapped into allowing their lives to be controlled by the real or imagined dictates of others. **An appropriate response:** *"I can't predict how anyone else might feel about it, but I like the idea myself."*

GUILT

Others' Emotions

"You hurt my feelings."
"You made me cry."
"You made me...(angry, embarrassed, unhappy, etc.)"

People sometimes react to our behavior with anger or other negative emotions. If they are unwilling to accept the responsibility for creating their own emotional responses, they frequently try to blame them on us. If we are unwise enough to accept their blame, then they have us right where they want us — willing to change our behavior to make them happy.

If we wish to avoid this unnecessary and unwarranted guilt, we must remember other people's emotional responses are caused, not by our actions, but by how they choose to react. They are at liberty to change their reactions whenever they like.

An appropriate response to these emotional accusations: *"It's unfortunate you chose to respond like this."*

"You've offended me."
"I demand you apologize."

Some people take offense just to make us feel we owe them something. They try to make us feel bad, so we will adjust our behavior to suit them. Since others' reactions are a matter of choice, if they decide to feel upset, it is not our job to convince them to behave otherwise. When anyone demands an apology from us, it is plain he desires to control us. Besides this, making an apology at another's insistence is a wasted effort all around because apologies extracted in such a fashion are worthless.

An appropriate response to all these emotional accusations: *"I acknowledge that you're offended."*

Lack Of Consideration

"How could you do that to me?"
"You ought to be ashamed of yourself!"
"See what you made me do!"
"I don't understand why you do these things."
**"I wouldn't have...(done this) if you hadn't
...(done that)"**
"You should have known!"

These statements and questions direct a barrage of guilt and criticism at us for being inconsiderate. In some cases, it is because other persons believe we were instrumental in causing them to decide on an unwise course of action. In others, it is because we have done something to which they object. Remarks like these are prompted by the speaker's desire to manage our behavior and make it more like what she believes it should be. These phrases and sentences imply that in one way or another, as far as being considerate is concerned, we have fallen down badly on the job. **An appropriate response:** *"You must believe I should have acted differently."*

"It wouldn't hurt you to...(do what I want)"

Whoever says this is not stating a fact but their belief. For all they know, what they are asking may be extremely distasteful from our point of view.

People who make statements like this imply we should be willing to do anything they want us to, so long as it doesn't cause us any physical damage. By phrasing their request in this manner, they try to put us in a position where we feel we must prove it *will* hurt us if we wish to avoid falling in with their plans. Just the fact that something will not hurt us is a poor reason for doing it. From the manipulators' self-centered perspective, their wanting us to do something is vastly more important than our not wanting to. This phrase is just another way to say, "Your discomfort is unimportant to me as long as I can get you to do what I want." **An appropriate response:** *"It might not hurt me, but I choose not to do it."*

The Test Of Love

"If you (really) loved me you'd..."
"If you thought anything at all of me you'd..."
"You don't love me. If you did, you'd...(be willing to do whatever I want you to)"

People who use these kinds of phrases are usually strangers to love themselves. They don't see it as a genuine, deep caring for another but as a handy tool for controlling people's behavior. It is a safe bet people who make this kind of statement are less concerned about love than they are with what they can get us to do for them. **An appropriate response:** *"You have some interesting ideas about love."*

Great Expectations

> **"I was hoping you would..."**
> **"I thought it would be nice if you..."**
> **"I expect you to..."**
> **"Don't let me down."**
> **"We have great hopes for you."**
> **"We've lived our whole life for this moment."**
> **"We want you to make us proud."**

These statements seem pretty straightforward, but each is a declaration of what others expect of us. By stating their desires in this manner, people try to incite in us a willingness to please them, coupled with a sense of obligation, so we will feel we must turn their expectations into reality.

Those who try to manipulate us in this subtle fashion fail to take two facts into account: first, we have no obligation to make their expectations materialize, and second, we have *our own* expectations, which are not necessarily the same as theirs. If we are to be at peace with ourselves, we must do what is best for *us*, regardless of what others expect. **Appropriate responses:** *"If my plans coincide with yours we'll all be happy,"* or *"It's nice of you to include me in your plans but I'm not sure mine fit in with yours."*

Unfavorable Comparison

> **"Why can't you be more like...?"**
> **"What if everybody else behaved like you?"**
> **"Everybody knows *that*."**
> **"If it's good enough for everybody else, why isn't**
>   **it good enough for you?"**
> **"Most people would..."**
> **"We don't expect you to be as good as _____ but**
>   **you should do better."**
> **"Nobody else is complaining."**

Irrational statements and questions like these imply something is wrong with us because we are not like others, and we should feel guilty for daring to be different. By comparing us unfavorably with other persons and by making them sound like the good guys, the speaker is trying to make us feel so uncomfortable we will back down from our position and behave as she would like us to. Generally speaking, manipulative attempts like this are the worst reason in the world to change our viewpoint. **An appropriate response:** *"I enjoy being myself, even if means I am different from others."*

Misdirection

> **"It will do you good."**
> **"It would be good for you."**
> **"It's for your own good."**

These phrases are used by people who believe they have a keener insight into what is best for us than we do ourselves, so they try to get us to accept their judgement. By stating their beliefs impersonally they try to create the impression their suggestions are supported by either outside authority or their own superior wisdom. Nothing is wrong with considering others' opinions, of course. Once we have reached legal age, however, no one has the right to make these kinds of choices for us; if we let them, we forfeit the opportunity to learn from our mistakes. As adults, we must be able to determine for ourselves what is, or is not, good for us. When we are confronted with statements like these, it is helpful to remember two facts: *first,* other people see things from *their* point of view, not ours; *second,* no matter how well-intentioned they are, other persons often do not know what is best even for themselves, much less for anyone else. **An appropriate response:** *"I'm sure you believe that's true, but I'll have to make that decision myself."*

"Don't you think..."

People sometimes use this line to get us to support their opinions. Those who employ it are asking us to confirm what they believe. In effect, this question is not actually a question, but a statement, which in essence says, "This is what I think, and I expect you to agree with me." By phrasing it as a question, they make it more likely we will answer "yes." If people genuinely wanted our opinion, however, instead of reinforcement of their own, they would say, *"Do* you think...", which invites us to consider the matter and reply with an honest answer. **Appropriate responses:** *"No", or "I haven't given it any thought", or possibly even "Yes."*

Implying a Deficiency

"You should be satisfied with what you have." *(There are people who have less — why are you complaining?)*

"That's the way it's always been done." *(There's something wrong with you if you think it should be changed.)*

"You ought to know better." *(Why didn't you do it the right way, like I would have?)*

"You ought to be ashamed of yourself." *(You've done something I disapprove of.)*

"I can't believe you did this!" *(Why don't you behave like I expect?)*

"I've never heard of such a thing." *(You've behaved so oddly.)*

"I don't understand why you do things like this." *(You have an obligation to explain yourself to me.)*

"How could someone as intelligent as you do something like this?" *(By dumping both flattery and guilt on you I may get you confused enough to do as I want.)*

"Why don't you make something of yourself?" *(Why don't you live by my values and act in a way I approve of?)*

People use guilt-evoking remarks like these to put us on the defensive and make us uncomfortable. They make it sound as though we owe them an explanation for behaving differently than they expected us to. We don't, of course, and their efforts to extract an explanation from us are actually just attempts to convince us to avoid the same kind of behavior (and consequently, the "need" to explain to them) in the future.

Three Little Words

Three words gain special significance when used by manipulators — *should, ought,* and *must.* Manipulators employ them to add weight to their suggestions and requests, to make them sound less like their own opinions and more like directives issued by a superior power.

There are two kinds of "shoulds": The *should of probability* and the *should of obligation.* The *should of probability* is logical; if it is raining and someone says "If you want to avoid getting wet, you should wear a raincoat or carry an umbrella," she is implying that achieving a particular result (in this case, staying dry) depends on our performing a certain action. In other words, if we have a specific outcome in mind, we will have to do whatever is necessary to bring it about. As long as there is an obvious benefit to us associated with what someone says we should do, "should" is used non-manipulatively.

The should of obligation is another story altogether. When people use "should" in this sense, they make it sound as though it is our duty to perform a particular action, but they neglect to mention any benefit we will derive from it. For example, someone might say, "You should visit your mother at least once a week." This may be an excellent idea, but unless the speaker precedes this sentence with something like, "If you want to be sure she's in good health," he is simply stating his opinion and trying to pressure us into agreeing by inferring it is our obligation. Or perhaps someone says to us, "You should get your hair cut." Since the speaker does not preface his remark with "I think...", which would indicate it was only his opinion, the overall effect is that an absolute judgement has been pronounced; a higher authority, using the speaker as its spokesperson, has decreed we must have our hair cut. Often, we are inclined to accept statements like this as factual because those who make them sound impersonal and objective.

Verbal Traps In Summary

We have all seen drawings created to be optical illusions. When we change the perspective from which we view them or change the focus of our eyes, we see a different picture than the one we saw at first. In a way, a manipulator's manner of speaking is like these illusionary drawings, because it does not mean what it seems to. Obviously, it is not sensible or realistic to imagine a hidden meaning in everything people say to us. But if we listen carefully, especially when others' words urge us to action, we may discover what they say is designed more to conceal their purposes than to explain them.

*

INCREASING YOUR AWARENESS

Divide a sheet of paper into two columns. At the top of the left column, write "What I said," and over the one on the right, "What I should say to avoid manipulating others." Now, think of manipulative techniques you have used on others. If you can't recall any, list the methods used successfully on you. Generally, we tend to use the same procedures that work on us, on others. Keep writing as long as you can come up with different techniques.

In the opposite column, across from each of these behaviors, rephrase your remark to make it non-manipulative. Change your "You ought to..." to "I think you ought to..."

Change your "Don't you think..." to "I think... What do you think?" and so forth.

This exercise may be difficult at first because we have to point the finger of blame at ourselves and identify our own manipulative techniques. The benefit of doing this is twofold: first, after a little practice we will cease manipulating others, and second, analyzing these remarks in this manner will make us immune to them ourselves.

AFFIRMATIONS

If I want something from others, I ask them directly, rather than trying to manipulate them.

I accept that others generally consider their needs and desires more important than mine.

If I feel guilty when I don't do as others ask, I need to discover why.

I do not permit fear of others' disapproval to influence my behavior.

My actions do not have the power to cause others' emotional responses.

If I decide to do something, it is because I believe I should, not because others do.

I have no obligation to fulfill others' expectations.

I am a unique individual and unlike anyone else.

I am the best judge of what I should or should not do.

I listen carefully when anyone says I should or ought to do something.

* * *

16

Habits

"If we fall into a routine rather than make decisions anew each time, we can get mindlessly seduced into activities we wouldn't engage in otherwise."
ELLEN J. LANGER

*M*ISTAKEN BELIEF:

It is impossible to break some of my habits because they are stronger than I am.

HOW HABITS BENEFIT US

Habits Can Make Our Lives Easier

Many of our mental and physical activities each day are carried on almost entirely by habit. Habits are remarkable mental tools; they save time; they eliminate a monumental amount of boring detail from our lives; they allow us to turn complex tasks into simple ones and make it possible to perform many everyday jobs with little or no conscious attention, freeing our minds to think about matters we consider more interesting or more important.

Habits Simplify Complex Tasks

Can you imagine how difficult life would be if we were unable to develop habits? Without them, we would be almost as helpless as infants. No matter how many times we repeated an action, we would never become any better or faster at it; every time we did it, it would feel as unfamiliar as it did the first time. Since we *can* create habits, we are able to perform many actions without conscious direction. As a result, when we execute a simple task like brushing our teeth, it is unnecessary to think about every little detail. Instead, once we pick up the toothbrush and toothpaste, everything seems to happen automatically, and before we know it, our teeth are clean.

Habits Facilitate Our Choices

If we were required to make a conscious decision about each action we performed in the course of a day, we would spend far more time making decisions than carrying them out. We would lose a great deal of time making conscious choices about such unimportant details as which shoe to put on first, for instance, or which hand should hold our fork. As it is, once we have made the same decision about a particular situation a number of times, the choice becomes habitual. So, instead of having to decide whether we should put on the left or right shoe first, we put our shoes in front of us and miraculously, in seconds they are on our feet.

CREATING HABITS

How We Develop Habits

After we have performed a series of related actions a number of times, we eventually develop a pattern or routine for them. A good example is the simple act of washing our hands, something we ordinarily do a number of times each day. Because it is such a common activity, we undoubtedly consider it easy. However, what now appears to be a simple procedure seemed complex to begin with, because to complete the task, a lengthy series of separate actions must take place.

When we first learned to wash our hands, each step of the process was preceded by a conscious decision: do we turn the faucet to hot or cold? How much water do we need? Should we hold the soap in our left hand or right? Do we clean our fingers first or the backs or the palms? Which hand goes on top when we are rubbing them with soap? How long must we rinse? Which hand should turn off the water? Does the right or left hand reach for the towel? How long do we need to dry? These are just a few of the many options we had to select from to complete this relatively uncomplicated job.

If we made the same choices each time we washed, the subconscious level of our mind soon accepted those decisions as permanent. At this point, unless something out of the ordinary occurs, once we start the job, our subconscious mind carries it through to completion, even though we may be engaged in another activity such as talking. The decisions we originally made one at a time have been incorporated into a smoothly-flowing pattern we refer to as a *habit*. A habit then, is a frequently-repeated pattern of mental and/or physical actions resulting from decisions that were originally selected consciously but are now performed with little conscious awareness.

HOW HABITS CAN WORK AGAINST US

We Allow Patterns of Behavior to Overpower Us

Sometimes habits get out of hand and instead of being a help, become a hindrance. Habits assume control in a manner similar to a plot used in a number of science fiction stories. In these stories, a sophisticated computer develops a will of its own and an intelligence superior to that of its creators, then proceeds to do what it pleases, rather than what its creators wish. Like that computer, our habits sometimes seem to take on a life of their own. Rather than us using *them*, they seem to use *us*, and we find ourselves doing things we no longer have a desire or need to do but which we nonetheless feel compelled to continue.

We Establish Harmful Habits

Our subconscious mind is infinitely flexible when it comes to adopting new behavior patterns; it will accept any pattern we provide it without question. Unfortunately, it lacks the ability to distinguish good habits from bad, so it accepts those that harm us as readily as those that help.

Unaware of the ultimate results of our actions, we unintentionally create harmful habits. Ironically, some habits that now harm us seemed gratifying originally. Smoking, for example, instead of being the pleasure we once imagined it, can become a compulsion. For some of us, eating has made a similar transition; rather than remaining an enjoyable way to nourish the body, it has become habitual behavior we perform mechanically as long as there is food in front of us, even when we are no longer hungry.

Undesirable Habits
Can Affect Our Self-Esteem

Not surprisingly, unwanted habits have a damaging effect on our self-esteem. The sense of being in control of ourselves that is necessary to a healthy self-regard is absent when we permit habits to gain the upper hand. How can we feel we are in charge when deeply-entrenched, damaging habits seem to prove we are not?

When we let harmful patterns of action control us, we often feel weak, inadequate, guilty and embarrassed, not only because of the hold these habits have over us, but because we have been unsuccessful in our attempts to break them. Inevitably, destructive habits generate a corrosive conflict inside us, with one part of us wanting matters to change and another wanting things to go on as they have been.

WHY SOME HABITS ARE HARD TO BREAK

We Are Afraid of Change

Why do we cling to habits we know or suspect might be harmful? Because they are familiar and comfortable. Once we have established a certain pattern to our actions we are reluctant to change it, even if it is not particularly helpful. This is because we feel threatened by change, even when it will ultimately be to our benefit. Old, familiar habits seem secure and reassuring, while new ones can involve risk, uneasiness and discomfort. Odd as it sounds, we would often prefer to continue old, habitual patterns of behavior, *even though they cause us pain and are potentially dangerous*, than face the task of replacing them with new ones that are more beneficial.

Bad Habits Can Be Fun

Some undesirable habits are hard to break because we enjoy them and don't genuinely *want* to break them. If we derive pleasure from a particular activity, then no matter how harmful it might be, we may be reluctant to give it up. We may understand a certain behavior pattern affects us negatively, and it would be better if we *did* change it, but if we are not too uncomfortable with things as they are, we may not make an effort. Why should we? Unless we are convinced there are more reasons to give up a habit than to keep it, we will not voluntarily let go of something we regard as desirable.

Habits Cause Changes to Our Brains

A frequently overlooked reason why we find habits hard to change is that they cause physical modifications in our brain. These changes make it easier to follow an existing behavior pattern. To understand how it works, imagine we walk across a grassy field each day to school or work and always take the same route. After a few weeks we no longer have to walk through the grass because by continually walking on it we've worn it down and created a path. This is similar to the way repetitive actions affect the brain; when we follow the same course of action repeatedly, a physical pathway develops in our brain. This path becomes more pronounced with each repetition until finally it is so well-established we find it difficult to act any other way.

THE TRUTH ABOUT HABITS

Those of us who believe we are at the mercy of our habitual behavior make a common mistake: we think of habits almost as though they are independent entities with an existence of their own. It is this kind of thinking, as much as the habits themselves, that causes us so much trouble. By thinking in this manner, we attribute too much power to our habits and too little to ourselves. The more we consider undesirable habits as entities in their own right, the less we feel able to change them. But no matter how irritating, awful, debasing, harmful, or disgusting some of our habits might seem, *they exist only because we permit them to. We created them, and we can uncreate them.*

COUNTER-BELIEF:

I can change or eliminate any habit whenever I choose.

HOW TO BREAK UNWANTED HABITS

Making Progress By Going Backwards

Since a habit is nothing but a series of conscious choices we have allowed to become unconscious, eliminating it is simply a matter of reversing the process by which we created it. Instead of continuing to let our subconscious mind make the choices for us, we begin to make each choice consciously with full attention.

If we want to break the habit of overeating, for instance, rather than concentrating on conversation or some other distraction while we eat, we devote our attention to eating and become conscious eaters. Throughout our meals we mentally ask ourselves questions: do we want to continue putting the food on the fork? To place it in our mouth? Do we want to chew it? Swallow it? Have we had enough to eat yet?

If smoking is the problem, we become conscious smokers; we break the process of smoking into its smallest parts and make each one subject to our conscious approval, beginning with removing the cigarette from the package and ending only when we put it out.

Why does this work? It works because whenever we make any part of a habit subject to conscious choice again, we weaken it. By performing each of the habit's component actions consciously, as we did originally, we constantly create fresh opportunities to decide whether we want to continue with it. If we persist with this, we will reach the point where the habit is no longer a problem or disappears altogether.

How does this cause our habits to stop troubling us? We know we can create a path by walking over the same area many times. What happens to that path if we stop using it? It may take a while, but before long the grass has grown up again, and the path is nowhere to be seen. Similarly, the longer we avoid indulging an unwanted habit, the weaker its pathway becomes in our brain. Here, though, the comparison between the grassy field and our brain ends, because even though the mental path grows fainter through disuse, unlike the path across the field, it is never completely eradicated. It *does*, though, become so weak it no longer has any power over us.

Replace Old Habits With New

To make the transition easier, we need to remember not only nature abhors a vacuum, our mind does too. We will find it far easier to eliminate an unwanted habit if we replace it with a habit we *do* want. By requiring ourselves to make conscious choices, we create the opportunity to replace old habits with some that will work to our advantage. Instead of continuing to overeat, we can substitute the habit of chewing our food thoroughly, which will help our digestion and our waistline as well. Rather than continuing to smoke, we can practice deep breathing and improve our overall health by bringing a greater volume of clean air into our lungs.

Benefits of Getting Rid of Undesirable Habits

Making unconscious choices conscious again may feel uncomfortable at first because it disrupts old, established patterns of behavior. The advantages of eliminating unwanted habits far outweigh any temporary discomfort we might feel as a result of it. Besides this, as we become more conscious of our actions, some remarkable changes will occur:

- **We drastically reduce the number of repetitions of unwanted behavior.** Because we must consciously decide whether or not to make them, actions we perform with our full attention take longer than those we do merely as a matter of habit. As a result, we have less time available for repeating them.

- **We lessen the habit's harmful effects.** If we require ourselves to make a series of decisions before we swallow each forkful of food, we have the opportunity to monitor the physical sensations that tell us we have had enough to eat. This being true, we are much less likely to continue eating once we have had enough.

- **The habit grows weaker and less demanding.** When we disrupt an established habit pattern, the subconscious level of our mind recognizes we are reconsidering some earlier choices, and it is less insistent that we repeat the old behavior.

• **We become able to re-evaluate the habit objectively.** Once we are able to stand away from our habits, so to speak, we see them from a different perspective. Our feelings about smoking, for instance, may change when we discover how unpleasant cigarettes actually smell and taste.

• **Our self-esteem increases.** We cannot help but think more highly of ourselves as we increase our control over our lives.

We need not be stuck with the habits we have today because we are stronger than our behavior patterns. No matter how deeply entrenched a habit may be, if we sincerely desire to get rid of it, we will. Since habits begin in our minds, they must end there, too. There is no reason why we cannot replace any destructive habits with behavior that will work to our advantage.

The mind, it has been said, is a good servant but a poor master. It is up to us to decide which ours will be.

*

INCREASING YOUR AWARENESS

Think of a habit you'd like to break. At the top of a sheet of paper, write a description of it. Then draw a line from top to bottom, dividing the sheet into two columns. Write the word "FOR" at the top of the left-hand column and the word "AGAINST" at the top of the right-hand column. Now, under the appropriate heading, list every reason why you should or shouldn't continue the habit. Continue to add to this list throughout the next week. When you've finished it, you should have more reasons listed in the "AGAINST" column than in the "FOR." Sit down with this list twice each day and review the reasons for discontinuing the habit. Think about each item on the "AGAINST" side and how it affects you negatively.

Now pick another behavior pattern to replace the unwanted habit. On another sheet of paper describe the actions you plan to use to replace the undesirable behavior. List the benefits you'll receive from the new behavior. Then, relax and imagine yourself in a setting where you would previously have performed the unwanted habit. Visualize yourself performing the new, beneficial action instead. Repeat this visualization at least twice each day. Use one of the affirmations below, or create one to support your change. If you follow this procedure for several weeks, the new behavior will begin to feel as familiar and comfortable as the old. With continued practice, the old behavior becomes less and less appealing and eventually drops away. For this procedure to be effective, the habit must be one you must genuinely *want* to eliminate.

You may sometimes slip into the old pattern of action instead of using the new one. If you do, *don't* judge or condemn yourself for having behaved less than perfectly. Just observe your actions and correct them, if possible.

AFFIRMATIONS

I control my habits; they do not control me.
I replace unwanted behavior with actions that benefit me.
I eliminate unwise or undesirable behavior from my life.
I develop new patterns of behavior to take the place of any that harm me.
I created my habits, so I can uncreate them.
I take conscious control of my behavior.
When my habitual behavior harms me, I replace it with beneficial behavior.

✳ ✳ ✳

17

Unrealistic Expectations

"As our own conceptions come to fit reality better, action taken from these conceptions produces the effects we want, instead of the reverse."
ANDREW WEIL

"We misperceive the external world and our own deeper desires and nature, act in a way that is contrary to the realities of our situation, and reap the unpleasant consequences."
CHARLES T. TART

Two words describe our prevalent attitude toward life: *chronic dissatisfaction.* We are unhappy: with ourselves and with our family, friends, job, income, home, relationships, social life, wardrobe, and so on.

But *why* are we unhappy? Life has not been so ungenerous to most of us that we have been deprived of necessities like food, shelter, or clothing. Our discontent has its roots less in what we have than in what we believe we *should* have; in our unsatisfied longings, our unrealized ambitions, and our plans that failed to work out. Much of what we have expected from life has failed to materialize.

As usual, when we are unhappy, it is because of incorrect beliefs we harbor. In this case, it is our beliefs about what we have a right to expect.

WHAT WE EXPECT FROM LIFE

MISTAKEN BELIEF:

*Things should happen the way I want them to, just because
I want them to.*

We say, "Wouldn't it be nice if this happened," or, "It would be wonderful if that happened," or, "Wouldn't it be great if ..." We plan certain parts of our lives in great detail, deftly instructing reality as to what we expect of it. We create elaborate scenarios for the future about experiences we would like to have or situations we want to occur, like getting a new car, having a relationship with a particular person, or getting a raise or promotion.

At first we think how nice it would be if a particular thing we wanted to happen *did* happen. The more we think about it, the more appealing it becomes. Then we go from where it would just be *nice* to get what we want to where it is *important* we do. We create mental movies of our desires, vividly imagining ourselves driving our new car, involved in a relationship, or spending the extra money we got with our raise and promotion. Before we know it, getting what we want has progressed from being merely *important*, to being *essential*; not only do we *have to* have what we want, we have convinced ourselves it is rightfully ours. Then, having persuaded ourselves it is a life-and-death matter and existence will be scarcely bearable if what we want to happen does not, we sit back and wait for it to materialize.

This is where we make our mistake. Nothing is wrong with having dreams, or making elaborate plans for the future, or with exercising our imagination. We must keep in mind, however, that hardly anything takes place purely because we want it to. Certain results inevitably occur as the effect of specific actions; if we fail to perform those actions, our hoped-for results will probably not be forthcoming. Sitting around hoping our wishes will materialize is a waste of time; hope is a thief of the present and a poor substitute for effort. Once we have decided what we want from life, we are well-advised to support our decisions with action and take whatever steps are necessary to make *sure* we get it.

COUNTER-BELIEF:

Unless I am willing to put some effort, perhaps even a considerable amount , into making my wishes become reality, they probably will not.

*

MISTAKEN BELIEF:

I have a right to expect certain kinds of behavior from other people.

In our youth, we learned certain rules about relationships and how to treat others. Having accepted these precepts, we wrongly assumed others were brought up with a similar code of conduct. As a result, we expect other persons to:

- treat us fairly
- behave courteously
- be honest
- agree with us
- understand us
- behave rationally
- be considerate
- look out for our well-being
- help us when we are in trouble
- respond to situations the same way we do
- avoid making us angry, unhappy, or fearful
- avoid behavior we dislike

Because we anticipate this kind of idealistic behavior, we are angry, hurt, and disappointed when it is not forthcoming. We need to understand that it makes no difference how *we* believe people should act because they will behave as *they* believe they should. Life would be far more pleasant and agreeable if everyone acted thoughtfully and considerately toward everyone else. The sad fact is, they do not. True, *some* people were brought up pretty much as we were, and we are probably comfortable around them because we know what to expect. We may as well accept, though, that a substantial number of people will act in ways we find disgusting, impolite, thoughtless, inconsiderate, selfish, dishonest, or in some other manner disagreeable.

Other than trying to always associate with compatible people, there is little we can do about others' behavior. Insisting that people be different than they are will just make us more unhappy. Whenever it seems people are being unkind, our best bet is to remember they are not at fault for their behavior. All they are doing is playing the game by the rules — *as they understand them* — just like we do. Considering the amazing diversity of the people on this planet, it is inevitable our individual ideas of what is or is not suitable behavior will be equally diverse. How can we expect others to treat us fairly, if we disagree on what is fair?

COUNTER-BELIEF:

It is unreasonable to expect others to behave as I want them to because their concepts of appropriate behavior may be radically different from mine.

*

MISTAKEN BELIEF:

I should be able to have everything I want, provided I want it badly enough or am willing to work hard for it.

As children, some of us came to believe we could always get whatever we wanted. We reached this conclusion because we could usually convince adults to give us what we wanted, either by being extra nice or by throwing temper tantrums.

Eventually a time came when others grew less willing to indulge us. Some of us got stuck at this point in our development, and if we have been unable to find someone to support us, have been complaining about life's unfairness ever since. Others of us joined the ranks of those who decided hard work was the answer. We reasoned that putting forth a certain amount of effort guaranteed that whatever we wanted would sooner or later be ours.

Much as we might wish this were true, even the greatest optimist will have to admit life is seldom an orderly and systematic process. When we incorrectly assume our success is assured because we are willing to put forth a great deal of effort to achieve or acquire something, we may be setting ourselves up just to be knocked down. How a situation turns out depends largely on whether our expectations are based on facts and probabilities or on desires and fantasies. Even if we build our plans on solid reality, there is no guarantee what we want to have happen *will* happen.

At times, though, life seems chaotic; unexpected incidents may occur for no apparent reason. Sometimes, despite our efforts, things fail to work out as we wish. When they do, we respond with disappointment or outrage and complain we have been treated unfairly. What we neglect to take into consideration is that we had no guarantee matters would turn out as we wanted. Few things in life are 100% guaranteed. There are so many variables involved in our earthly existence that we cannot predict with any certainty what will, or will not, take place. True, hard work is usually a significant factor in realizing our ambitions, but it isn't the only one. Sometimes, like it or not, it is not enough.

COUNTER-BELIEF:

Neither desperate desires nor hard work guarantee I will always get what I want.

*

MISTAKEN BELIEF:

Life should be fair; there should be a limit to the amount of pain and unpleasantness I have to put up with.

To our way of thinking, life must always unfold pleasantly. We demand the course of events runs smoothly, and if something bad *does* happen, we insist it be no more than a minor inconvenience. Among other things, we expect the following:

- to always be well-fed and cared for
- to live comfortably
- to be able to do what we want
- to be able to go where we want
- to be right a large part of the time
- to be able to avoid change
- situations to work out as we want them to.

On the other hand, we require that we *not* be troubled by accidents, illnesses, unhappy relationships, deaths of close friends and family members, or any other event we would refer to as tragic, unpleasant, or awful. So when matters go as we want them to, we say life is *fair*. When they do not, we cry, "Foul!" and complain loudly about how terrible things are and how *unfair* life is.

Like so many other aspects of us, our standards of fairness are highly individual; they are our personal beliefs about what should or should not be allowed to happen. But just because we consider something fair does not mean others will. The thunderstorm that makes us postpone our picnic provides water desperately needed by farmers; for each person who wins, at least one other must lose; the store whose low prices put merchants out of business supplies goods to people who could not otherwise afford them. In other words, the terms *fair* and *unfair* do not indicate absolute values, only our approval or disapproval.

COUNTER-BELIEF:

Things are neither fair or unfair; they just are. These terms do not reflect the actual nature of an action or event, only how well it fits into my plans.

THE CAUSE OF OUR PROBLEMS

The common thread running through these damaging beliefs is this: we think life and other people should live up to our expectations. This is why we are so often disappointed and hurt. Our true problem, though, is not with life or other people; it is with what we *expect* of them. We have not based our expectations of them on reality, but on *unreality*, on ideas existing only in our minds. We have confused what we want with what we are likely to get; we have mistaken desirability for probability. We have constructed our future on a shaky structure of wishes, hopes, and dreams.

We Were Set Up for Disappointment

It is easy to understand why we have impractical expectations; we have been immersed in unreality since we were small. With the best of intentions, our parents taught us about Santa Claus, the Tooth Fairy, and the Easter Bunny. These generous make-believe characters gave us gifts in exchange for little or nothing on our part. We learned about God, whom we could petition for favors. If we were convincing enough and promised to behave, we were told, we might be able to persuade the Supreme Being to change Its plans for us in favor of our own. These and other fanciful ideas encouraged us to believe it was possible to get something for nothing.

Then, if we are typical products of our culture, we acquired other unreasonable ideas from dubious and unreliable sources, like popular songs, novels, movies, television, and advertising. In some of these imagination and reality were so skillfully blended that, as children, it was difficult or impossible for us to tell one from the other. Without the tempering wisdom of experience, we found it confusing trying to distinguish reality from fantasy.

Other distorted ideas came from the friends, teachers, and authority figures who helped shape our lives. Their concepts of life were usually more realistic than the products of the advertising and entertainment industries. Nonetheless, a certain amount of their irrational thinking rubbed off on us. After being primed in this fashion, it is not surprising we ended up believing we lived in a world where dreams came true almost by magic and where wishes were sometimes granted merely for the asking.

THE INEVITABLE RESULTS
OF UNREALISTIC THINKING

As a result of this thorough grounding in unreality, rather than observing reality and developing expectations based on what we have observed, we make up rules and expect reality to obey them. Then, when circumstances fail to develop as we wish, as they often must, instead of recognizing that we played a part in making ourselves unhappy, we blame reality for being as it is.

The problem, however, is not with reality. It is with our resistance to it. We have the false, destructive belief that matters should always go our way, and we should not have to put up with anything we don't want to. Like small children, we are sure if we complain loudly enough and long enough, someone or something will come to fix things for us. So we beg, pray, and demand. We whine, protest, and criticize. We cry, scream, kick, and stamp our feet, which, of course, makes no difference.

Unrealistic Expectations = Emotional Pain

If we think about it, we will realize practically all our emotional pain occurs in response to situations that turned out differently than we thought they should. Some of us, because our hopes are so far removed from what is likely or reasonable, could not make ourselves more miserable if we intentionally set out to. Despite the fact that they usually end up disappointing us, amazingly enough, we go on creating the same kinds of unreasonable expectations. This is especially strange since, as adults, we *know* events do not happen by accident; we know everything is caused in one way or another and that it makes no sense to demand things be otherwise.

THE TRUTH ABOUT REALITY

It is to our advantage to acknowledge that reality will often be different than we want it. No matter how much it displeases us, people *will* go on acting in ways we dislike, and unpleasant situations *will* continue to occur. Disliking or objecting to situations outside our control will not make them go away; we cannot beat reality into submission if we are not particularly happy with it. If we continually tell ourselves how terrible things are, sooner or later we will become so depressed we will feel even less able to deal with them than before. It will pay us to remember that while we are not required to *like* everything that goes on, we *do* have to accept it.

How to Stop Resisting Reality

What can we do to overcome our resistance to the realities of life? The wisest and healthiest policy is to simply take matters as they come, recognizing life will sometimes be as we want it, and other times it will not. To lessen our unhappiness, we need to stop judging the world by how we would like it to be, instead of by how it is. When we learn to accept whatever comes our way, we will find *events are bad only if we interpret them as such.* Of greatest importance to our peace of mind is that we firmly grasp that *it is not reality that needs to change, but our attitude toward it.*

What can we do when things are not to our liking? We can take a closer look at situations we dislike, to discover how we helped create them. We can realize our disappointments are not personal affronts but feedback telling us to think matters through more realistically. Invariably, there will be times we are unhappy but can do nothing to change what has happened. When this is the case, an objective assessment of the circumstances, *untinged by negative emotions,* will often make us aware of new and even better options than were available originally. Then having taken these steps, if there is something we can do to improve the situation, let us do it and if not, direct our attention elsewhere.

Cooperating With Reality

Some things can be changed, and others cannot; to a great extent, our happiness depends on how well we can distinguish the first category from the second. Once we stop fighting life and start working with it, we will realize that, based on the law of cause and effect, matters are the only way they can be at the present time. If we want them to be different, then *we* must be instrumental in making them that way. When we say, "I don't like the way things are," let us add, "Let me see what I can do to change them."

Future Happiness

All we can say with any certainty about the future is, no matter how carefully or cleverly we plan for it, there will be things we both do and do not expect. This seems tragic only if we believe having absolute control over every aspect of our lives is a key ingredient for happiness, which it is not. Nothing is wrong with simply waiting for life to reveal itself as it is, or with just letting circumstances develop naturally, instead of trying to force them to mesh with our preconceived notions.

Once we stop making so many demands about what *should* happen, we will be much happier with what *does*. Keeping our expectations in line with reality will not lower our standards or make our lives less enjoyable; it will just make us more relaxed and happier. Even if events do not always happen as we have planned them, the world is still a delightful place to live. And reality, once we become accustomed to cooperating with it, can actually be quite pleasant.

*

INCREASING YOUR AWARENESS

A Reality Check For Your Expectations

At the top of a sheet of paper, write the word "Expectations." Beneath it, leaving a left margin of an inch, make a list of events you expect to occur in your life. This can include items you would *like* to have happen, those you feel *should* happen, and those you believe *must* happen. They can relate to any part of your life — school, home, work, social life, relationships — anything at all that has any significance to you. For instance, you might *like* to get a new job, or you feel people *should* be nicer to you, or you believe you *must* get an "A" on your math test. Use as many sheets of paper for this as you like.

Separate these expectations into three groups. In the left margin, classify each of them by writing "**1**" to indicate you believe it would be *nice* if it happened, "**2**" if you think *it's important* that it happen, or "**3**," if you think it *absolutely must* happen. Having done this, take the one you consider of greatest importance in category **3** and write a brief description of it at the top of another sheet of paper.

Now ask and answer the following questions about this expectation:

1) *Is what I want to have happen actually possible?* Has the same sort of thing happened for or to other people? They don't necessarily have to be people you know personally. If others have experienced essentially the same thing you wish to have happen to you, at least you know it can be done. This moves your expectation from the realm of imagination to that of possibility.

2) *Is it a fairly common occurrence?* Does what you want happen to many people or on a fairly frequent basis? Or does it only occur infrequently or to just a few people? If it is common, your chances of achieving it are increased, and if not, they are slimmer. Remember: although many others have experienced a particular thing, there is no guarantee *we* will.

3) *Are there more reasons why it should take place than why it shouldn't?* Just wanting badly for a particular thing to happen doesn't count because hardly anything comes to you just because you want it desperately. Unfortunately, sometimes we want something so much we ignore the many reasons we are unlikely to get it. If there are more reasons something should *not* take place than reasons it should, it probably will not.

4) *Does what you want depend primarily on you to bring it about, or does it depend mostly on other persons or nature?* If what you want requires the cooperation of either nature or one or more

others, chances for success are lessened considerably. Both people and nature are notoriously unpredictable, and if either of these variables is in your equation, the accomplishment of your goal is far less certain than if you were relying on only yourself.

5) *If there are practical steps you can take to make your desire a reality, are you prepared to take them when necessary or already taking them?* It would be wonderful to just lean back and wait for what you want to come your way. Usually, though, the pleasant, enjoyable parts of life come to you only in return for a certain amount of effort on your part. Unless you are willing to put your energy into making a particular situation reality, it will probably remain only an expectation.

The more of these questions we can answer "yes," the more likely our chances of success because we are building our expectations on a solid foundation of reality. With every "no," however, our chances of disappointment increase because an important part of the foundation is absent. If our expectations have little in the way of fact about them, then we must be extraordinary persons with exceptional determination to bring them about.

There are two times this exercise is particularly effective: when you first decide you want a particular thing to happen, and when something you wanted to happen, hasn't, and you feel disappointed. Following this procedure will keep both your life and expectations better grounded in reality.

AFFIRMATIONS

I willingly accept life as it comes even if I do not like it.

I have no realistic choice but to accept what is.

I choose to feel good no matter what circumstances come my way.

I accept everyone, including myself, unconditionally.

I willingly accept what is.

I accept that it is often impossible to control other people or circumstances.

I avoid resisting unwanted realities I am unable to change.

I am not harmed by what happens, only by my resistance to it.

I cease resisting things I am powerless to change.

I am flexible; I can adjust to any circumstances that face me.

It is unreasonable to expect people to behave as I wish, just because I want them to.

Life is neither fair nor unfair - it just is.

When life is different from how I want it to be, I change what I can and accept what I cannot change.

I accept reality as it is.

✳ ✳ ✳

18

Negativity

"...be ye transformed by the renewing of your mind..."
ST. PAUL

"Men are disturbed not by things but by the views they take of them."
EPICTETUS

*M*ISTAKEN BELIEF:

Certain occurrences and events are negative by nature.

WE *DO* WANT TO BE HAPPY....DON'T WE?

Would you rather be happy or unhappy? This question probably sounds foolish because everybody wants to be happy, don't they? Strangely enough, although we all *think* we want to, numerous times each day when we have the opportunity to choose between happiness and unhappiness, we *choose* to be unhappy! Perhaps a friend is late for an appointment, and we become angry, or we accidentally spill something on our clothing and become upset. Maybe the boss yells at us, and we become apprehensive about losing our job, or the person we have been dating for several months has not called lately and doesn't answer our messages, and we feel anxious and afraid.

We interpret actions or circumstances like these negatively; we consider them bad, awful, tragic, fearful, terrible, serious, and so forth; we apply unpleasant labels to them to illustrate how horrible we believe they are.

Are Painful Feelings Natural?

"Wait a minute," you may say, "feelings like these *are* normal; they are natural. *Everybody* reacts like this when bad things happen to them." True, negative feelings are *normal*, in the sense that the majority of people feel them at times, but they are far from natural. They may feel that way because we have experienced them for so long, but to be natural they must be built-in responses we're born with, unchangeable parts of our biological mechanism, and they are not.

HOW NEGATIVE EMOTIONS AFFECT US

Does feeling bad about a situation make it any better? Definitely not — it makes it *worse* because no condition is ever improved by being looked at negatively.

Negative Emotions Limit Our Viewpoint

Unpleasant emotions have a paralyzing impact on our mental processes; they short-circuit our thinking and cause us to make inappropriate choices and decisions. When we respond to a situation negatively, we don't address the actual problem; we just mindlessly repeat subconscious behavior patterns we learned earlier in our lives, which do nothing to resolve it. By reacting to problems in this mechanical fashion, we neglect the opportunity to address them consciously and creatively and forfeit the chance to solve them and learn from them as well.

Negative Responses Can Harm Us Physically

If we experience intense anger or fear, our sympathetic nervous system mobilizes our bodies to fight or run. It does this by, among other things, secreting adrenaline, causing our hearts to beat faster, and sending an increased flow of blood to our muscles. In this manner it prepares us to protect ourselves from physical danger, despite the fact that our problems are generally emotional or psychological in nature. Once we've generated this energy, it has to be expended in some manner. Unfortunately, we most often release it by engaging in inappropriately aggressive behavior toward others or by turning it inward on ourselves, creating a condition generally referred to as *stress*. If we continually subject ourselves to stress, we open the way for any number of psychosomatic illnesses, including ulcers, high blood pressure, headaches, asthma, eczema, hives, and psoriasis.

Negative Emotions Are Rarely Productive

Does approaching situations negatively make them easier to deal with? Not at all. In fact, unpleasant feelings are more likely to *prevent* us from attaining our objectives than to help us because negative feelings are counterproductive. When we look at our problems from a negative viewpoint, we decrease our chances of finding workable solutions. Instead of solving problems, a negative attitude perpetuates them. When we have convinced ourselves a certain kind of situation is bad, we seldom attempt to look at it positively, and consequently, we are unwilling to admit it has any good aspects.

HOW WE LEARNED
TO BE NEGATIVE

Observing others' actions as we were growing up, we noticed certain situations seemed to provoke specific emotional responses; people became angry when one kind of situation occurred and unhappy in response to another. To our youthful eyes it appeared as though the circumstances caused the feelings. So to fit in with others and not draw unfavorable attention to ourselves, we patterned our behavior after theirs and began reacting as they did whenever we were involved in similar situations.

It is this "monkey see, monkey do" attitude that causes us to respond to death with grief, to loss with sorrow, to frustration with anger, to uncertainty with apprehension, to indifference with hurt, to lack of excitement with boredom, and so on. So, rather than natural, these unhelpful attitudes are learned reactions, habitual patterns of behavior we use to respond to situations we interpret as actually or potentially harmful.

But isn't it appropriate to feel bad about some things? Isn't it normal to grieve about the death of a loved one? In some cultures, yes, even among individuals who profess belief in an afterlife, because grief is customary behavior under such circumstances. In others, no; some societies consider death a liberating experience, a welcome transition that allows people to transcend earthly restrictions and embark on a more joyous, more fulfilling existence. To persons in these societies, a loved one's passing is reason for rejoicing and celebration, not for sorrow.

THE FACTS ABOUT OUR RESPONSES

What is the truth about the situations or experiences we've learned to believe are negative? Although we are inclined to think certain occurrences must automatically trigger unpleasant emotional responses, it is not true. There may be times when circumstances appear so serious it is hard to imagine there could *be* a lighter side, but *no* event or action is intrinsically or inherently negative. Every occurrence is essentially *neutral* in character — neither positive *nor* negative. Events only *seem* good or bad because that's how we've learned to interpret them.

If we decide a particular event is horrible, we collect data to support that belief, and it does, indeed, seem horrible. On the other hand, if we decide it is agreeable, we gather evidence to support *that* belief, and the event takes on the nature of a pleasant occurrence. In other words, *we can make anything seem like either a benefit or a disaster, depending on the attitude we adopt toward it.*

COUNTER-BELIEF:

I can reframe any apparently negative occurrence or event and derive positive benefits from it.

There is nothing — absolutely nothing — that does not have positive aspects as well as negative. If the favorable features are not readily apparent, all we need to do is look for them. Since they are always there, we can choose to emphasize those instead of less helpful ones. This may seem difficult to grasp at first because it is so different from what we have come to believe, but it is no less accurate for its strangeness.

We have all heard the old story about the pessimist referring to a partly-filled glass of water as half-empty, while the optimist describes it as half-full. A pessimist will say, "This situation is awful!", while an optimist says, "How can I make this situation work to my advantage?" What is an optimist, anyway, but someone who has made a habit of finding positive benefits in every situation, who refuses to accept negativity as the only answer?

Being Positive Isn't Playing Make-Believe

We may think, "Aren't we just fooling ourselves if we do this, pretending things are different than they actually are?" Emphatically, **NO**. Deception is unnecessary. What we are doing is exploring the neglected, but equally real and valid, *positive* side of the situation. It is neither necessary nor desirable to fool ourselves into believing certain circumstance have no unfavorable aspects because that would make us view matters unrealistically.

But what if a situation *does* have unpleasant aspects? Is there any point in dwelling on them and ignoring the *good* ones that can work to our benefit?

Some people have the idea a particular kind of event is tragic so firmly fixed in their minds they refuse to entertain any ideas to the contrary. Does it make sense to insist something is awful when it makes us miserable? Does any clear-thinking person choose to be unhappy when he need not be? Since the option of selecting a positive perspective is always open, why should we subject ourselves to the pain and discomfort of a negative one?

This is not to say people do not have the right to respond negatively if they choose to, or to deny that people *do* suffer from unpleasant emotions. Of course they do. The point is, they do not *have* to; the pain resulting from negative responses is totally voluntary. If, being aware better alternatives are available, we *do* decide to respond negatively, it is as though we are offered a choice between bread and a rock when we are hungry, and rather than choosing the bread to nourish us, we content ourselves with chewing on the rock.

What it amounts to is this: we have a choice; we can interpret circumstances negatively **or** positively. Since there are obvious benefits to taking the positive approach, why should we look at matters any other way? After all, no law says we *must* react negatively to certain kinds of situations; we do so only because of habit and custom.

ACCENTUATING THE POSITIVE

What if, for instance, our car broke down and we were unable to get it fixed right away? How could a problem like this have a bright side? Under these circumstances what could we do?

Let's explore some options. We could say, "This is terrible; this is awful — I don't know what I'm going to do. How will I ever be able to get by without a car?" This would make us feel wretched and get us absolutely nowhere. What happens, though, if we look at this situation constructively?

> • If we don't have to go anywhere, we can take advantage of being at home to do some projects we have been putting off for lack of time.
> • We may try walking or biking to our destinations and find it is not only good for our health but enjoyable too.
> • This may be the perfect opportunity to look for a new car, something better and more reliable.
> • We might total our automobile expenses for a year and realize we could save a lot of money by using public transportation instead of making car payments and paying for insurance, gas, new tires, repairs, and maintenance.
> • If we try riding the bus to work, we may decide we like it because we can read or relax, instead of becoming tense driving in heavy traffic each day.
> • We might decide this is a good chance to check out some local specialty stores we've ignored in favor of larger ones further away.

Maybe the situation we are having trouble with is losing a job. We may feel somewhat insecure not knowing where our next paycheck is coming from. However, many of us dislike the jobs we have now, so perhaps this might be a good time to look for one we *do* like, maybe closer to home, in more attractive surroundings, or better-paying. Regardless of what kind of situation we face, when we become aware we are thinking negatively about it, we can decide to ignore the old interpretation in favor of a more resourceful one.

Change May Feel Strange

If deliberately substituting positive attitudes for negative seems artificial at first, don't be surprised. Since we are in the habit of thinking a particular way about situations, reversing our attitude will conflict with our normal habits of thought. Also, because our thoughts have had their own way for so long, our attempts to impose order on them may meet with some resistance.

Any feelings of strangeness, though, are only temporary. Changing thinking habits is just like learning any other skill, such as tennis, or dancing, or driving a car: it takes a little time and effort to begin with, but once we have the knack, we can immediately put it into practice. All it takes on our part is a decision to make the change and the persistence to carry it out. As we proceed with the process, we will realize it is not only less grim than we thought, it can even be fun. Ultimately, we will find any discomfort we experience because of this change will be more than offset by its long-term rewards.

HOW A POSITIVE
APPROACH BENEFITS US

We Can Assume Control Of Our Lives

Being able to interpret events to our advantage puts us in control; we realize it is unnecessary to accept defeat, feel victimized, or feel we are at the mercy of unfavorable circumstances. By taking advantage of the positive aspects of a situation, we take control and make it work to our benefit. Regardless of what goes on around us externally, even if we are enslaved or imprisoned, having absolute control over our thoughts can make our inner world a place of freedom.

We Can Make Our Emotions Work For Us

Although we may doubt it at times, we live in a friendly, supportive world. If at times it seems otherwise, it is because of how we interpret what happens to us. Since our thoughts are directly related to how we feel, when we change our interpretation to emphasize the positive aspects of events, our feelings about them change, too, and increase our happiness. By choosing how to react, we choose how we feel.

Negative Interpretations Make Us Feel Bad

Depending on the use we make of it, our ability to interpret events as we wish can be either the biggest curse or the greatest gift we have. When we tell ourselves a particular situation is awful or tragic and make a negative judgement about it, our bodies stop producing endorphins, the naturally-occurring biochemicals that make us feel good about life. Not only do we not feel good when this happens, we begin to feel *bad*.

A Positive Attitude
Improves Our Problem-Solving

Without exception, there is a light and a dark side to everything. Taking a positive approach to a situation opens our minds to opportunities and beneficial aspects we would probably ignore because we were busy concentrating on how awful things were. It stands to reason that as long as we remain focused on a situation's unpleasant features, we will be oblivious to those of a positive nature. By directing our attention to the advantageous features, we can demonstrate, as others have, that problems can be exploited to our benefit, disadvantages can work to our advantage, and debits can be turned into assets.

We Have the Opportunity to Change Our Responses

Some of us may be concerned we will become emotionless if we down-play the negative facets of life, but this is not what happens. On the contrary, we experience as much emotion as always but with a significant difference; it will be noticeably happier and filled with more love, creativity, and satisfaction in achievement than ever before. Granted, we will experience fewer *unpleasant* feelings, but that is a gain, not a loss.

We Can Create a New Life for Ourselves

Psychologists Willard and Marguerite Beecher have said, "In truth, happiness has no causes. It is a decision — which can be made consciously or unconsciously — on the part of the individual that life is worth living, even though it is less than perfect."

Happiness begins and ends in our minds; we are happy or unhappy not because of what happens but because of what we *think* about what happens. As Shakespeare said in *Hamlet*, "There is nothing good or bad but thinking makes it so." The liberating truth is **nothing in the world is awful or horrible,** *unless we arbitrarily define it as such.* We do not have to think negatively about *anything,* no matter what we have been told, what others believe, or how we have responded in the past. We are free to react constructively, instead. Since that option is always available, what point is there in responding otherwise?

As we can see from observing those around us, some people's lives are predominantly pleasurable; this is not an accident. By changing our outlook, **ours can be, too.** While it may be impossible to alter the course of events, we *can* change our attitude about them, and that is what truly matters. Continually looking at life's light side will make our future rewarding, pleasant, and comfortable. As a wise man once said, "It is not the universe that needs improving, it is our way of looking at it."

*

Increasing Your Awareness

(You will be more successful with this exercise if you begin by using events that troubled you only mildly. Take your time about working your way up to more painful experiences.)

Draw a line down the center of a sheet of paper. Above the left column write "**Negative Interpretations,**" and above the right, "**Positive Interpretations.**" In the left column list something that recently happened to you which you consider bad or painful. Write what your thoughts were at the time. Now think of some positive aspects of the same situation, and write them in the right column. If you habitually respond negatively, it may be difficult at first to come up with positive ideas about things. If this is true of you, use *any* positive aspect of the situation to counter the negative impressions, even things which seem silly or trivial. It is not the impressiveness of your ideas that is important, but your ability to switch to a positive viewpoint. When you've finished with this incident, move on to another one.

You will find using this exercise half an hour each day for a week will start changing your focus. With continued use, looking at occurrences constructively will become a habit and provide you with a more positive, creative frame of mind. Remember, this exercise is not something we do just to make ourselves feel good; we also do it to gain a more accurate, objective look at reality because reality is neither positive nor negative.

Affirmations

I choose to see each incident in my life as beneficial to me in some way.
I choose to emphasize the positive aspects of every situation.
How I respond is always my choice.
It is not what happens that causes me pain but my interpretation of it.

I take responsibility for making the world a happy place for myself.
I am willing to enjoy life.
I enjoy being alive.
Since I control my thoughts, I can decide to think positively about anything.
My happiness is not caused by people or events outside me; I create it myself.
I refuse to become upset about matters outside my control.
My happiness depends on me.

* * *

19

Solving Problems

"... a puzzle is a problem that we usually cannot solve because we make an incorrect assumption that precludes a solution."
RUSSELL L. ACKOFF

*M*ISTAKEN BELIEF:

The people and conditions in my life are the source of my problems.

There are three kinds of people, we are told: those who *make* things happen; those who *watch* things happen; and those who wonder, "What happened?" To express it differently, there are:

1) persons who consider themselves the victims of circumstances and believe there is little they can do about it;

2) people who try to adjust themselves to fit existing circumstances, and

3) people who use their initiative to create circumstances favorable to themselves.

These attitudes represent the three basic levels of self-esteem. Nowhere do we reveal the status of our self-regard so clearly as we do in our approach to resolving difficulties. To show how our feelings about ourselves affect the way we handle problems, let's take a situation that could happen to anyone and try to reach a satisfactory solution using each of these strategics.

LISA AND SUSAN

Lisa McCallum worked in the advertising department of a large computer manufacturer. One morning the department head, Mr. Prentice, had everyone in the department meet in his office. The purpose of the meeting, he explained, was to inform them the firm was planning a special advertising campaign to introduce their newest, most powerful computer. According to Mr. Prentice, instead of having the staff pool their ideas as they usually did, the company's president would select the theme for the ad campaign from entries submitted by employees in the advertising department. The person whose idea was chosen would be put in charge of the project and would receive a substantial cash bonus. Prentice went on to tell them their ideas were to be submitted in writing by the 12th, and the winning entry would be posted on the bulletin board on the 16th.

When Lisa arrived at work on the 16th, she felt excited. She knew the idea she turned in was excellent, and she fully expected to be the winner. But when she checked the bulletin board, she was shocked; Susan Rawlins was the winner! Susan's idea was much like Lisa's, except Susan had elaborated on it.

It suddenly occurred to Lisa that Susan must have copied Lisa's idea. She remembered the day she returned from lunch and found Susan leaning over the desk on which lay Lisa's notes about the project. Lisa recalled having heard some office gossip about Susan, gossip hinting she might have done the same kind of thing before. Lisa was perplexed. Unfortunately, she had no proof the idea was originally hers. Under the circumstances, what could she do?

SOLVING THE PROBLEM

Although there is only circumstantial evidence to suggest Susan stole Lisa's idea, let's assume Susan Rawlins *did* copy Lisa's idea. What would be the most effective way to deal with this problem to eliminate the likelihood of it happening again?

LEVEL ONE SOLUTIONS

The Helpless Victim

Lisa wondered if **it might be best just to forget about it because probably nothing would be done anyway.** When we respond to situations like this with resignation, it is primarily because we doubt our ability to resolve them in our favor. Since our position seems hopeless, why even make an effort? Our past experience leads us to believe our attempts to straighten out the matter would be wasted because nothing would come of them. By taking no action, we confirm our belief that we are powerless victims who never know what kind of crisis might devastate us next.

When our self-esteem is this fragile, we feel incapable of facing problems directly. We don't feel we are *in control* but that we are *being* controlled. To us, the earth is a hostile planet in an unfriendly universe, where one disaster after another overwhelms us and where others get the lucky breaks while we get stuck with the rotten deals.

The Vindictive Victim

Rather than take this lying down, Lisa decided on a different tactic. **She would say nothing to anyone, but she would plan a way to get even.** This attitude is a slight improvement over feeling hopeless because she would be taking action, rather than just feeling sorry for herself. Reacting in this fashion, though, will do little except relieve emotional tension because our goal would not be to make right, but to retaliate. Since we have no concrete proof Susan is guilty, for all we know, we might be planning to avenge ourselves on someone who is totally innocent! From the standpoint of ethics, if we *were* to behave in this fashion, our actions would be no better than we believe Susan's to be. Seeking revenge might harm Susan or cause her inconvenience, but it would do nothing to solve the problem.

Both these possibilities are dead-end solutions. They permit us to avoid confronting the problem directly, but because they do, we forfeit the opportunity to solve it. If we select either of them, we respond from weakness rather than strength. If we assume the part of the **Helpless Victim,** we passively accept whatever happens. What would be the result of taking the role of the **Vengeful Victim**? Then, instead of *acting,* which might improve the situation, we would be *reacting,* by trying to create as much pain for someone as we believe she has created for us. We resort to answers like these only if we believe there is no possible way to correct a problem.

Probability of success of Level One solution: *None*
Likelihood of problem reoccurring: *High*

LEVEL TWO SOLUTIONS

The Complaining Victim

Lisa reconsidered. She decided the other two solutions would be ineffective, and besides, they would not make Susan aware *Lisa* knew what Susan had done. There were, she knew, several other options. **She could go to her boss and tell him she believed Susan stole her idea and that she had heard similar rumors before.** She realized, however, even if Mr. Prentice did intervene, she was without proof to support her accusation. Since it would be strictly her word against Susan's, she ruled out that answer.

The Angry Victim

Still seething at the injustice of her predicament, **she thought about telling Susan, in no uncertain terms, exactly what she thought of someone who would pull such a dirty trick.** With her temper out of control, though, she knew she would probably do herself more harm than good, so she wisely decided against it. Telling Susan what she thought of her might allow her to let off some emotional steam, but it would bring her no closer to a solution.

The Vengeful Victim

Realizing her emotions were clouding her judgement, she thought it might be best to calm down first, **have a quiet conversation with Susan, and tell her if anything like this happened again, Lisa would make sure everyone in the company knew what kind of person Susan was.** Almost as quickly as the idea came to her, she decided against it. She had only suspicions to back up her accusation, and that was not enough ammunition with which to confront Susan. Besides, she realized, this type of approach was more likely to end in a name-calling match than to provide a satisfactory answer.

Why did Lisa decide these answers would probably not work? While the actions of the **Complaining Victim** and the **Angry Victim** might provide some emotional relief, neither was likely to generate positive results. The biggest obstacle to the success of Vengeful Victim's solution was that it required Susan to behave differently than she would ordinarily. If a problem can be solved only by getting others to change their behavior, we had better be prepared to offer them a positive incentive, or they are unlikely to cooperate. Level Two solutions provide only *negative* incentives: fear of authority; avoidance of another's anger; threat of exposure. While avoiding these kinds of hazards can be a powerful inducement, Lisa's position was so weak none of these strategies were likely to do her any good.

Probability of success of Level Two solution: *Low*
Likelihood of problem reoccurring: *High*

THE LEVEL THREE SOLUTION

The Non-Victim

Lisa felt thoroughly confused. She had come up with a number of possible solutions, but none of them sounded like they would work. What else *could* she do? "Just a minute," Lisa thought, "am I looking at this situation the wrong way? Maybe it is not the *answer* I need to change, but the *problem.* Could it be **the problem is *not* that Susan stole my idea but that *I was careless in leaving the information lying around where others could see it?*"** Lisa was right.

*C*OUNTER-BELIEF:

People and conditions do not cause my problems; I cause them myself.

Reframing the problem will not clear up the matter of Susan taking Lisa's idea, but with her newfound wisdom, Lisa accepts this as the price for her carelessness. She has realized it is often more important to take steps to prevent a problem from reoccurring than to resolve the immediate situation in our favor, a matter of losing the battle but winning the war. By understanding it was within her power to keep this kind of situation from happening to her again, Lisa eliminated countless future problems.

None of her first answers would have been effective because she defined the problem incorrectly. She had seen it as being that of Susan stealing her idea. That was actually a *secondary* problem, however, brought about by the existence of a primary problem — her carelessness in leaving her materials around where anyone could see them. If she eliminated the primary problem, the secondary problem could never reoccur. Only by defining the problem correctly was she able to find an effective, permanent solution which required no one to change but herself.

On reflection, Lisa realized it was unrealistic to expect everyone she worked with to be honest. Since there was no way to give every person she associated with an honesty test, she could not be 100% sure of their honesty. This being the case, she decided her best bet was not to assume people were *either* honest or dishonest — but to keep an open mind until circumstances proved them to be one or the other. By doing this, she prepared herself for either possibility and eliminated this kind of problem from her future.

Probability of success of Level Three solution: *High*
Likelihood of problem reoccurring: *Low to non-existent*

HOW SELF-ESTEEM AFFECTS OUR PROBLEM-SOLVING SKILLS

Seldom do any of us solve all our problems from the same level. This is because we are more willing to admit to weaknesses and shortcomings in some areas than in others. Generally, though, it is our degree of self-esteem that determines first, if we will try to solve the problem at all, and second, the level from which we will approach it.

Level One Solutions

If our self-esteem is low, we often decide upon a Level One approach. Those of us who operate from this level incorrectly think many problems are unsolvable. Often, this is because we have been told so by individuals whose own dismal failures seem to provide abundant proof of it. Because this belief encourages us to sidestep problems rather than face them squarely, we lack experience in problem-solving and, consequently, have limited faith in our abilities.

Level Two Solutions

If we have moderate self-esteem, we usually select Level Two solutions. When we operate from this level, we believe many of our problems *can* be solved — but only with others' cooperation. That is why problem-solving efforts on this level so often fail. While Level Two solutions sometimes require a degree of flexibility on *our* part, it is usually *others* we expect to make the greatest changes. Even if they agree to alter their behavior to humor us, any changes they make will often be only temporary, unless we are prepared to offer them desirable incentives. If our solution requires others to alter their behavior to make it work, there is a good chance it will fail.

Level Three Solutions

Solving a problem from Level Three requires us to *first*, accept the blame for the problem ourselves, and *second*, to make a change in our actions or beliefs to eliminate the problem. Consequently, only those whose self-regard is high enough so they do not feel threatened by either self-criticism or change will choose it. But solutions arrived at from this level are the only ones that will give us permanent relief from problems. If we approach them from either of the other levels, we run the risk they will never be solved to our satisfaction.

*

ACCEPTING RESPONSIBILITY

OUR GREATEST PROBLEM

The biggest problem facing our civilization is not war, hunger, poverty, or disease. Nor is it any of the other commonly mentioned problems we hear about daily in the news. Instead, it is our refusal to accept responsibility for our own lives. Whether as individuals, communities, cities, or nations, our unwillingness to be held accountable for what happens to us is at the root of the social ills that threaten not only our civilization but the entire world. It is this reluctance, whether on an individual or global basis, that makes smokers with lung disease blame tobacco companies, intoxicated drivers blame the cocktail lounge that sold them alcoholic beverages, and the rest of us blame anyone or anything but ourselves for our misfortunes.

Why We Blame Others

Why is there an almost universal need to blame our problems on others? Simply put, because few of us like ourselves well enough to accept the blame. We feel threatened if we have to admit to any kind of fault. If we do, there is danger our already inadequate self-esteem will shrink even smaller. If we can convince ourselves *others* are the source of our unresolved predicaments, however, we can point the finger of blame at *them*, instead of toward ourselves. While steadfastly ignoring our part in the problem, we can insist it is *their* obligation to solve it. On the other hand, if we acknowledge we had a part in creating it, then *we* have to change.

Blaming Others Doesn't Work

It is tempting to think that if people would just behave as they should (meaning the way *we* want them to) there would be an end to our problems. The truth is, the responsibility for our problems is primarily ours. *We have always had the power to avoid many problems ourselves because the choices and decisions leading up to them have been ours all along.*

THE SOLUTION

It is not that we lack the wisdom and understanding necessary to solve our problems. We already have them; we have been looking in the wrong direction for their solution. Rather than searching all around us to detect their cause, we need to direct our attention closer to home. We need to realize we are a *cause*, not an *effect:* that our lives are under *our own* control; that *we* possess the power to avert many difficulties; that problems do not just "happen," they happen because of what we do or, in some cases, don't do; that our problems generally begin *inside* us, instead of *outside*, and since that is where they originate, that is where we must solve them. Instead of saying, "Look what he did to me!" we must learn to feel comfortable saying, "What could *I* have done to prevent this?"

When a problem confronts us, the first thing we must do is assume we caused it. This is not always true. It *is* true much of the time, though, and only if we assume it is will we start looking for ways *we* can solve it. When faced with a problem, we need to ask ourselves, "Is there any reasonable action I could have taken to prevent this?" With an open attitude like this we can usually trace our involvement back to where a different action on our part would have kept the problem from happening. We do this detective work not to make ourselves feel guilty but to discover the part we played in the problem. By doing so, we obtain the solution. This may not help us solve the immediate problem, but by understanding how we contributed to a problem, we learn how to avoid it in the future.

When, by a shift of perspective, we grasp that *we, and not others, cause our problems,* we will no longer waste time looking for solutions that require other people to change their behavior.

Instead, we will be like the person who said, "I wondered why somebody didn't do something; then I realized I *was* somebody."

Accepting Personal Responsibility

What does it mean to accept personal responsibility? It means whenever we have an unhappy experience, we look first to ourselves to see how we might have caused it, and only after determining our past actions were not its source, are we free to look for a different culprit. It means giving up the role of victim in exchange for accountability and the knowledge that we, and no one else, are responsible for our lives and well-being. It means increasing our awareness of the price we must sooner or later pay for our actions. It means although we may not realize or *like* it, we cannot escape the consequences of everything we think, say, and do. It means realizing that when our lives are out of control, we are the only ones who can restore them to order. Finally, it means we can exchange bitterness, anger, and frustration for the peace, happiness, and satisfaction that are ours when we deliberately take charge of our lives.

We have not completed the transition from childhood to adulthood until we stop saying, "It got broke," and learn to say, "I broke it," instead. When we do, we gain an incredible feeling of freedom because we realize the solution to most of our problems lies in our own hands. We will experience this feeling and know we are free when we cease blaming anyone or anything outside us for our unhappiness.

*

INCREASING YOUR AWARENESS

1) Recall a past situation in which you were victimized, greatly inconvenienced, or experienced a severe problem. Now, find out how you could have prevented it by assuming you *did* cause it. To do this, follow the situation back in time, step by step, until you reach a point where a different action on your part would have kept the problem from occurring.

Let's say, for instance, you were driving on a freeway and became involved in an accident when one of your tires blew out. Now, without thinking about anyone else's part in the situation, what could *you* have done to have prevented this from happening? One solution, of course, would be to avoid driving altogether by staying home or by taking some kind of public transportation. This would definitely eliminate the possibility of the problem recurring, but for many of us, it is impractical. The simplest solution would be to check the condition of your car and tires at regular intervals. This would not *guarantee* you would avoid further accidents, but it would decrease the chances.

If you follow this procedure regularly, there will be times you conclude you could only have avoided a particular difficulty by going to ridiculous or unreasonable lengths. Don't dismiss these ideas out of hand. Even if you decide against taking a drastic step that would help you avoid specific problems, you will at least be aware you have put yourself at risk by *not* doing so. Being aware of this makes you better prepared if problems *do* occur.

AFFIRMATIONS

I am totally responsible for my own life.
I am in charge of my life.
I accept full responsibility for my life and well-being.
I cease blaming others and solve my problems by understanding my part in them.

I am in full charge of my life and affairs.

I am responsible for everything I do, say, or think.

I accept the consequences of my actions.

I accept responsibility for my mistakes and problems.

I am inescapably responsible for everything I do.

I regard every problem as an opportunity to improve the quality of my life.

If I have problems, they occur because I still have more to learn.

I can improve my life permanently by discovering how I cause my problems.

* * *

20

Looking Up

*M*ISTAKEN BELIEF:

I must look up to certain persons because they are better than I am.

We believe we have to "look up to" certain persons or respect them because they are superior to us in one way or another. We single out those in particular occupations, such as doctors, lawyers, and other professionals, for our admiration. We respect clergymen because we believe they are morally superior. We honor elected officials because they hold important and powerful positions. We idolize media stars and famous athletes for their abilities. We defer to people we believe are above us in specific ways, who seem smarter, better-educated, wealthier, or who have a "higher" social standing.

In part, we developed this attitude because our parents encouraged us to respect people of whom they were in awe. In part, we acquired it because as children we felt so helpless anyone bigger or more powerful seemed thoroughly deserving of any homage we paid them. And finally, we accepted this belief because it went unchallenged by the same persons to whom we gave our honor and respect. Many of them, with self-esteem problems of their own, soaked up our applause like a sponge absorbs water. By accepting our admiration so willingly, they conveyed to us that it was no more than their due; their position or their accomplishments gave them special status and set them apart from the rest of us. If we were willing to offer them praise, they were not about to refuse it.

HOW BEING RESPECTFUL AFFECTS US

Our response to believing certain others are above us depends on our self-esteem. Some persons who consider themselves below others regard the situation as purely temporary; given enough time, they believe, they will equal or surpass those they now feel are above them. Others, who are close observers of human behavior, gradually and sometimes painfully come to realize their idols are only human like everyone else. Those of us who think so little of ourselves that we do not challenge this incorrect idea are in danger of continuing this useless, demoralizing adoration till we die.

Its Effect on Our Self-Esteem

How does believing some people are perpetually "above" us affect our self-esteem? In the only way it can — destructively. By accepting others' superiority as fact, we place ourselves in a *deficiency relationship* with them. We acknowledge they have something we do not and believe we owe them respect because of it.

By continually putting ourselves down this way, we become second-class citizens. If we think others are more important, then we must be insignificant; if we believe them to be superior, then we think of ourselves as inferior; if we regard them as smarter, then we consider ourselves as more ignorant; if we think they are capable, then we judge ourselves inept.

We cannot look up to people unless we think we are beneath them. It is something like being on the teeter-totters or see-saws we played on as children: the only way we can elevate those on the other end is by putting ourselves lower than they are. As long as we believe there are persons we must "look up to," then we will look down on ourselves.

The Difference Between Us

Why is it wrong to use criteria like this to judge people or to determine their value, because their wealth, attributes, or occupations *do* set them apart from the rest of us.

True, certain people stand out because they are superior in one way or another. But these distinctions are not valid criteria by which to judge anyone's human worth. Occupation, education, wealth, talent, skill and social standing are purely *artificial* standards that we and others like us have created and endorsed as legitimate. By using them to judge ourselves and others we imply that human value can be based on external attributes, when it cannot.

We Are Equally Deserving of Respect

It is not that people like those we have been talking about do not *deserve* respect — of course they do. The point is, *we are all equally deserving of respect* and no one of us more so than any other. Although external distinctions like skills, position, or title may make people *different* from us, in no way do they make them any *better* or more deserving of respect. No matter how different we may be on the outside, on the *inside*, we are all the same.

COUNTER-BELIEF:

I have as much intrinsic worth as anyone else and am equally deserving of respect.

Parting Is Such Sweet Sorrow

There is a certain amount of sadness and reluctance involved in letting go of our idealized images of others. No matter how we idealize them, however, the people we have always thought of as "above" us are just ordinary human beings. They eat, drink, and sleep like we do. They perform the same bodily functions in the bathroom. And just like us, they have colds, runny noses, and stomach gas and, on occasion, can be disagreeable, thick-headed and foolish.

While an attitude of worshipful admiration may sometimes be proper for a child, it is unsuitable for an adult. Mature persons do not look *up* at people or *down* at them; they simply look *at* them, because in terms of human worth, we are all the same.

*

INCREASING YOUR AWARENESS

1) Using a sheet from your notebook, make a list of people you look up to. Write each one's name, followed by the reason you consider her or him superior to you. These don't have to be lengthy explanations - just enough to serve as a reminder. If it's a teacher, for instance, you might write "his education," or a physician, "her medical knowledge," or a wealthy person, "his

riches, " or a member of the clergy, "her unselfish attitude." (Since we receive mixed messages throughout our lives, you may discover you admire contradictory qualities, like wealth and unselfishness, or power and humility.)

When your list is complete, think about the first person on it and about the quality or trait you admire. Then ask yourself, "Does his being different from me in this respect make him *superior* to me, or does it just make him different?" Continue this procedure with each name on the list, and repeat this daily for at least a week. When the week is up, review your earlier assessments. Do they seem as valid as before?

2) If you are in the mood for detective work, on another sheet of paper write the names you used in the first exercise, skipping a line after each name. On the line following each name, write who originally told you to look up to this person. Once you have figured this out, ask yourself this question: "Was the person who told me this ever wrong about anything?" Depending on your answer, write either, "This person was always right," or "This person was sometimes wrong and could have been wrong about this," after that person's name.

AFFIRMATIONS

My worth as a person is as great as that of anyone on earth.
All persons, including myself, are equally deserving of respect.
High positions, titles, degrees, or achievements do not add to anyone's value or importance.
No person is inherently more valuable, worthy, or deserving of respect than any other, including me.
I give the same honor and respect to myself that I give to others.
No one is superior to anyone else because of his or her achievements.

*No matter how different others are from us externally, in terms of
    inherent worth, we are all the same.*
I look neither up to nor down on others — we are all equals.
Regardless of title or position, no one is higher or lower than I am.
No one is more important or less important than I am.

* * *

21

Religious Beliefs

"Irrevocable commitment to any religion is not only intellectual suicide; it is positive unfaith because it closes the mind to any new vision of the world. Faith is above all, open-ness — an act of trust in the unknown."
ALAN WATTS

"The most formidable weapon against errors of every kind is Reason. I have never used any others, and I trust I never shall."
THOMAS PAINE

*M*ISTAKEN BELIEF:

God may be offended if I question any religious beliofs.

THE ACCURACY OF
OUR RELIGIOUS BELIEFS

We Hesitate to Question Spiritual Beliefs

Although we consider numerous aspects of our lives open to question, typically, our religious beliefs are not among them. Discussing or even thinking about spiritual matters makes some of us uneasy or afraid because we have an almost superstitious veneration for them. To some of us, even *contemplating* challenging religious beliefs seems sacrilegious. We are afraid God might become insulted or angry and punish us if we are irreverent enough to question what we have been told is His word.

We did not arrive at this attitude by ourselves. Usually, it was fostered by those responsible for our religious upbringing. Although we have been encouraged to apply logic to most areas of life, we have been told to throw it out the window when it comes to religion. It is as though we believe God at some time said, "Well, go ahead and apply logic to anything *else* you like, but don't try it on spiritual matters. I'll be deeply offended and upset if you even *think* of approaching them rationally."

Beliefs Were Presented As Facts

Unless we were raised in an exceptional family, religious beliefs were not presented as matters open to question or discussion but as accomplished facts. If we accepted them, it was usually not because they made much sense, because they seemed true, or because they seemed to have any practical application. It was because those who parented us made it clear they expected us to accept them or made us think we might incur severe, long-term penalties if we did not.

As a result, we have accepted certain beliefs about spiritual matters, not because we *know* they are true or because they are logical or reasonable, but simply because others told us they were true or convinced us it was wise to adopt them. The worst part of this situation is the people who assured us of the accuracy of these beliefs do not know this from their own experience. All they can do is testify they were told certain beliefs were true by people who did not themselves know they were true but who believed they were because they had been assured of it by others, who had been told by others, who in turn had been told by *still* others, and so on. In other words, as far as the validity of certain religious beliefs is concerned, *no one alive knows for sure they are true.* Despite people's insistence that their religious beliefs are accurate, they are unable to support their contention with the tiniest shred of proof.

There is a party game called, among other names, "Rumors." To play it, people first form a line, and whoever is at the end of the line thinks up a sentence or phrase and whispers it to the person next to her. That person whispers it to the person next to him, and this continues until the message has reached the other end. Then the person on the other end repeats what he believes he was told, and the originator repeats the original message, so everyone will know what was said to begin with. The starting and ending messages usually differ greatly, and the contrast between the two is often humorous.

The purpose of referring to this game is just to illustrate what can happen when information is transmitted from one person to another over even a short period of time. This is not to say any particular religious belief is incorrect as a result of having been conveyed in this manner. It is merely to point out that, with as much reliance as there has been on persons passing beliefs on to others, there is a substantial margin for error.

HOW RELIGIOUS BELIEFS AFFECT OUR SELF-ESTEEM

In his penetrating study, *Man, The Manipulator*, psychologist Everett Shostrom characterizes a manipulative (and consequently harmful) religion as "one that stresses the inability of man to trust his own nature. If he cannot trust his own nature, he needs some external religious system... The role of [this kind of religion] is to keep man more like a helpless child who constantly needs the help of ministers and priests."

Considering the great variety of religions, the many denominations, faiths, sects, cults, and forms of worship that exist, and the vastly different and often contradictory beliefs they espouse, it is inevitable some of them will have a more positive effect on our self-esteem than others.

With this in mind, let us look at how various kinds of beliefs affect us.

A belief affects our self-esteem negatively if it:

> • encourages us to worship a god who is less understanding and forgiving than we are ourselves;

> • causes us to experience negative emotions, such as guilt, fear, or anger, or makes us think negatively about ourselves or others for any reason;

> • teaches us we are evil and sinful simply as a result of being born into this world. Some persons who believe they are unworthy try to burden us with the feelings of sinfulness and shame they experience themselves. If we lack self-esteem, we may buy into their beliefs and adopt a faith that represents God as harsh, demanding, and almost impossible to please. If we consider ourselves essentially bad and unworthy, then we see nothing strange in worshipping a deity who will administer the punishment we believe we deserve;

> • allows us to deny responsibility for our actions and blame them on powers or forces outside us. It is tempting to believe injuries, diseases, and problems are inflicted on us by external forces because that relieves us of the need to be accountable for them. If we *do* believe this, life seems chaotic and unpredictable, and we needlessly feel like victims;

> • urges us to think the world is an evil place and to postpone enjoying life now in the hope of greater rewards after death. Those who are convinced the only purpose of earthly life is to qualify or disqualify us for future rewards try to persuade

us of this. If we let them, we fail to live fully in the present;

• advises us God's ways are not for us to question or that we are incapable of understanding God's motives. If we attribute everything we do not understand to the "will of God," we will not try to discover the actual causes of certain events. If this attitude were common, mankind would have made little progress fighting disease, hunger, and ignorance during the past centuries;

• instructs us we need an intermediary to approach God on our behalf because we are unworthy. Those who want us to believe this often have a vested interest in the matter because *they* are the intermediaries on whom they urge us to rely. We may fall prey to this belief if we have a poor self-image because we consider ourselves inadequate. It was not the Supreme Being who came up with this idea, however, it was *man*.

• advises us to condemn others because - they are in some way "different." Beliefs like this encourage intolerance — first of others, *but eventually of ourselves;*

• persuades us we are superior to others because their religious beliefs are different from ours. No one benefits from playing "My god's better than your god." It is pathetically easy to delude ourselves into believing we are "superior" to others when we create our own definition of the term.

A belief affects our self-esteem positively if it:

• emphasizes that our nature is essentially good and that we are acceptable and lovable just as we are, faults and all;

•encourages us to accept responsibility for all our actions, *including the mistakes.* If we believe we will experience the consequences of everything we do, we will try to make our actions will benefit others as well as ourselves;

• teaches us all people are equally deserving of respect, regardless of how different from us they might be;

• instructs us that in God's eyes, *no* sin is unforgivable, and the key to forgiving others is to first learn to forgive ourselves;

• tells us the world is neither good nor evil in itself but is the kind of place we make it;

• urges us to act on our own initiative to achieve our goals, rather than waiting for divine or supernatural intervention;

• provides us with a positive frame of reference through which we can view ourselves, others, and the world. The emotions of love and joy stimulated by this kind of belief are good for our self-esteem and our psychological health.

THE IMPORTANCE OF PROOF

We have been told we must accept certain religious beliefs on faith. But why? Only in the area of religion are we expected to believe so much with little or no evidence to support it. It is small wonder unquestioning faith is a requirement for the acceptance of numerous doctrines because it is impossible for anyone to prove they are correct.

Why should we accept others' unsupported word? It is neither sensible nor psychologically healthy to unquestioningly accept *anything* is true without reasonable verification. Religious beliefs, because the element of superstition sometimes creeps into them, should be subjected to even *closer* scrutiny than other beliefs. It does not serve us to blindly accept whatever is told us, no matter who tells us or how exalted their titles. When it comes to matters of the spirit, it is not only our right to ask for proof, it is our *responsibility.* When people tell us we should believe something, we need to ask: "How do **you** know this is true?" It is immaterial that those who urge us to accept certain tenets sincerely believe them themselves because sincerity has never yet been proof of accuracy.

Doubt and Skepticism Are Healthy

It is perfectly OK to doubt what everyone else believes, even in regard to religious matters. When something is true, it cannot be harmed by doubt. If it were not for those who doubted, either because they viewed matters differently than most or disbelieved what others insisted was true, we would not have the great variety of world religions we have today.

What do Martin Luther, John Wesley, Mary Baker Eddy, Mohammed, Buddha, and Jesus have in common? The fact that they were all doubters who were unhappy with the religious status quo of their times and who, *because* of their doubts, ended up revitalizing religion rather than damaging it. Martin Luther, especially, must at times have experienced grave doubts about his right to challenge existing church doctrines. Was it actually possible, he must have wondered, that *he* was the only man in Christendom who was right, and everyone else was wrong?

COUNTER-BELIEF:

Our honest skepticism is less likely to offend our Creator than our refusal to use our reasoning powers to discriminate between the true and the false.

There is no reason to avoid using our judgement and reasoning abilities to examine ideas about religion. The Intelligence which created us endowed us with excellent mental faculties, and there is nothing to indicate we must exempt *any* beliefs, *regardless of their source or nature,* from the careful scrutiny of those abilities. We were not blessed with the magnificent reasoning powers we have only to ignore them when in regard to matters of the spirit. Every area of our lives should be open to examination. To set aside certain beliefs as too sacred to question is to live in unnecessary, self-imposed ignorance and to deliberately close our eyes to the truth.

It is wisest to be like Ralph Waldo Emerson, who said:

> "He who would gather immortal palms must not be hindered by the name of goodness, but must explore if it be goodness. Nothing is at last sacred but the integrity of our own mind."

*

AFFIRMATIONS

It is my right to doubt whatever I choose.
I maintain a healthy skepticism to make sure what I believe
* is true.*
I accept full responsibility for my actions, rather than blaming them
* on anyone or anything outside me.*
I apply my intelligence and reasoning powers to every part of my life.
I keep an open mind on all subjects.

*I do not accept everything others tell me just because they insist
it is true.*

*I reserve the right to make my own decisions on all matters,
regardless of their nature.*

*I reject all attempts to make me believe I am inherently bad or
sinful.*

* * *

22

Helping Others

"...you should not be guided by your own ideas of what is good for others. A man who claims to know what is good for others is dangerous."
NISARGADATTA MAHARAJ

*M*ISTAKEN BELIEF:

It is my obligation to help people who seem unable to take care of themselves.

Nothing is wrong with helping others with their problems. In fact, there are many reasons we *should* be helpful. On the surface, the idea of providing assistance when others need it seems admirable. But is it? When we step in to solve others' problems, are we in fact helping, or are we just fooling ourselves and harming them in the process? It is commendable to aid those who are handicapped physically or mentally, or by the inexperience of youth or the infirmity of old age. And even the best-prepared of us need help occasionally because of unforeseen problems. Despite our good intentions, though, helping others can be destructive, to both us and them. Too often people see our compassionate help

236

as encouragement to continue the behavior that made it necessary in the first place.

SOME PEOPLE ABUSE
OUR WILLINGNESS TO HELP

Most problems do not appear mysteriously for no reason; people cause them, usually by acting unwisely. While it is one thing to perform an action out of ignorance of its consequences, it is quite another to anticipate negative repercussions and proceed with it anyway. Ideally, once people understand how they cause their problems, they will make the appropriate corrections, and the problems will stop occurring. Sometimes, however, those who wish our help are not much interested in preventing their problems or in solving them either. Why should they be, when it is so much easier to bring them to us?

Why do others so often rely on us to solve their problems? They do so because people who continually receive help eventually become accustomed to it. They begin to think it is their right and come to expect it, either from friends and family or from the government or social service organizations. As long as they can convince others to resolve their difficulties, their problems cease being problems as far as they are concerned. They get along nicely, thank you, manipulating others into taking care of them.

HELPING CAN
ENCOURAGE DEPENDENCY

We Have Been Trained to Be Helpful

It was impressed on us early in our lives that it is our duty to help others, so when people have problems, we customarily feel sorry for them and ask if there is anything we can do to help. When people seem defenseless, we are supposed to stand up for them. If they get in a financial bind, we should be willing to lend them money. When they feel low, it is our responsibility to cheer them up. If they face difficult decisions, it is our obligation to advise them. When they are at the end of their resources, we are expected to make ours available. If someone picks on them, we must stand poised and ready to defend them. In short, we must be prepared to remedy others' shortcomings or deficiencies, even at some expense to ourselves. As noble as these sentiments sound, though, indulging them can have a damaging effect on everyone concerned.

Co-Dependency

People who enjoy feeling relied on sometimes enter into a relationship with another person who likes to be taken care of, creating an alliance known as *co-dependency*. For this type of arrangement to be mutually satisfactory, the "strong" participant must be able to feel good about himself as a result of solving the other's problems. The "weak" member of the team must appear helpless and defenseless, so the "strong" member can step in, rescue her, and make everything right again.

This may sound like an ideal relationship because the participants' needs seem to fit together as neatly as the pieces of a jigsaw puzzle. In fact, this sort of arrangement cripples everyone involved. Although one player in this little drama appears to be stronger than the other, in truth, *both* participants are weak. The person who relies on someone or something outside himself to give him feelings of self-worth is as dependent as the one who seems unable to solve her own problems.

HOW HELPING CAN DAMAGE SELF-ESTEEM

Unnecessary Help Can Lower Others' Self-Esteem

Unless we are adults making decisions for children, it is arrogant to believe we know what is best for others. When we wade in with both feet to solve people's problems and act as a buffer between them and reality, our well-meant efforts often do more harm than good. Our caretaking conveys the message that we help them because they are inept and unable to care for themselves. The resulting feelings of inadequacy further damage their already-fragile self-esteem and reinforce their belief they are helpless and incapable of successfully resolving their difficulties.

Problems Have A Purpose

To a certain degree, a person's feelings of self-worth depend on his ability to not only solve his problems, but to avoid creating them in the first place. When we solve others' problems, we take away their chance to develop problem-solving skills of their own. By cushioning them from the consequences of their actions, we deny them vital opportunities to learn from their mistakes. Unless we grant individuals the chance to experience firsthand the results of their errors in judgement, they will go on behaving unwisely, creating even more problems in the future. Only by facing their problems directly can people discover the role they played in creating them and, in doing so, learn how to avoid causing similar problems in the future. Eventually, persons who get themselves *into* scrapes must learn how to get themselves *out* of them. The sooner they are allowed to do this, the better for all concerned.

By assisting others in remaining dependent, we encourage them to believe in fantasy. We permit them to pretend the law of cause and effect does not apply to them, that it is possible to get a free ride, to do whatever they want without having to pay for it. As long as we let them persist in the illusion that someone will always be around to pick up the tab or bail them out, they have little incentive to mature and develop problem-solving abilities of their own.

Our well-intentioned interference in their affairs gives others a false sense of security. It permits them to postpone, but not escape, the inevitable. None of us can avoid the consequences of our actions (or inactions) indefinitely. Unfortunately, others' unwillingness or inability to solve their problems now is likely to cause them even greater problems in the future. When they are finally forced to face life on their own, they will find themselves mentally and emotionally ill-equipped to handle it.

How Helping Others
Can Harm Our Self-Esteem

It is easy to fall into the trap of dependency, to feel good about ourselves because we help others. First, because some people are willing to accept all the help we will give them, no matter how little they need it. Second, because our government and our society encourage dependency, it is so commonplace we think little of it.

A dependency relationship among adults is unhealthy and unavoidably damaging to self-esteem. It can persuade us to base our good feelings about ourselves on service to others, as though self-esteem is something we must earn rather than our birthright. Too, the good feelings we get from assisting others are only temporary; they must be continually reinforced. If we just feel good about ourselves when we aid others, how will we feel when we become the persons who *need* the help, rather than those who give it?

Some of us, if the truth were known, do not actually *want* to help those whose only genuine need is to learn to help themselves. Because of the injunctions we learned as children, we find it difficult to ignore others' pleas for help, even though we may be fully aware they need assistance only because of their own indifference. Too often our early training prevails and convinces us we have a moral obligation to help, and we should feel guilty if we do not. Then, because we feel as though we are being pressured into doing something we dislike, we feel manipulated and resentful. So we forfeit some self-respect because we *know* we are being imposed on but not how to prevent it.

AVOIDING
DEPENDENCY-RELATED HELPING

What about those of us who wish to avoid the snare of dependency? The only solution is to set our own guidelines for helping. Otherwise, it will be difficult to know whether we are actually helping others or just making it easy for them to avoid looking for their own solutions. If we are satisfied our help is given to people who are unable to obtain it through their own efforts, we can feel pleased to give it, as pleased as we would feel if the situation were reversed, and we were the ones on the receiving end. Compassion, understanding, and an ability to imagine yourself in another's place are part of high self-esteem. These characteristics allow us to provide freely given and genuinely supportive help to those who, through no fault of their own, are incapable of helping themselves.

It is not our job to eliminate the stumbling blocks in others' lives; they are there for a purpose. Nor is it our duty to help others by trying to compensate for what we consider their deficiencies. Neither is it our responsibility to fund an endless round of handouts, whether of time, energy, or resources, to people who are only unwilling, not unable, to help themselves. There is no reason to feel compassion for people who have the knowledge and ability to change their condition but elect not to.

*C*OUNTER-BELIEF:

I am under no obligation to help those who are capable of taking care of themselves.

It is up to us to wean those who needlessly depend on our help. Withdrawing aid from them may seem heartless, but regardless of how it appears, it is the kindest thing we can do. It may build our ego to help others with their problems, but when people are capable of standing on their own two feet, we do not help them by supporting them, we *harm* them. Until we refuse to give them further assistance, they will go on living unrealistically, creating problems and expecting us to solve them. And why not? As long as we continue to reward them with our support, they have no incentive to change their behavior.

HOW WE *CAN* HELP OTHERS

There are many ways we can provide aid to others *without* doing things they can and should be doing for themselves. We can teach them how to solve their own problems, instead of solving them ourselves. We can help them learn to take care of themselves by assisting them in developing their *own* skills and abilities. We can cease protecting people who are perfectly capable of looking out for themselves. We can stop supporting people who are well able to care for themselves. We can avoid making dependency easy by providing them with excuses ourselves. We can offer them love and encouragement and give them recognition for their accomplishments. And finally, we can demonstrate the value of self-sufficiency with the best example of all — our own lives.

We need to be sharply aware of the difference between the kind of help that makes someone stronger and the kind that encourages further dependency. When we love people, we do not do what will make *us* feel good unless it is also what is best for them in the long run. If we genuinely love others and are not playing dependency games, we do not deprive them of the opportunity to think and do for themselves. It is a far better indication of our love that we *stop* solving their problems and give them the opportunity to mature by correcting their own errors.

When we are tempted to protect other persons from the consequences of their actions, we need to remember no one has given us the right to determine they should not be allowed to learn from their mistakes. Unless we permit people to cultivate their self-reliance, we give them no genuine or lasting help. True compassion does not lie in merely alleviating others' suffering but in showing them how to eliminate suffering in the first place. Ultimately, the most beneficial help we can give others is not our continuing assistance but the freedom to grow and develop on their own.

*

INCREASING YOUR AWARENESS

(Please bear in mind these questions are not posed with the intention of dissuading you from helping those who are genuinely in need of help: the old, the young, those with physical or mental handicaps, those who have problems through no fault of their own, or those whose care is legitimately your responsibility.)

Here is a series of questions to help you decide, on a situation-by-situation basis, whether it is wise to help others. You can apply it when you are uncertain about your motives for helping. To use it, write "Help or Harm" at the top of a sheet of paper. Write the numbers 1 through 9 down the left margin of the sheet. Now ask yourself the following questions and put either "Y" for "yes" or "N" for "no" next to the corresponding number on the paper.

1) Do you feel you become a better person by helping others?
2) Do you enjoy feeling needed and depended upon?
3) If you saw other persons providing the same kind of help you're thinking of giving, would you consider them unwise?
4) Have you helped this person with one or more similar problems in the past?
5) Does the person who wants help seem to need others' help often?

6) Is your help likely to encourage the person's dependency?
7) Is your help likely to harm this person in the long run?
8) Is this something they would be better off learning to take care of themselves?
9) Are you thinking of helping because you're afraid the person asking for help will become upset or think poorly of you if you don't?

If you have more N's than Y's, your urge to help would seem to be based more on genuine need than on misplaced sentiment. On the other hand, if the Y's predominate, you might do well to give the matter further thought.

AFFIRMATIONS

I do not have to put others' needs before my own.
I allow others the opportunity to learn from their mistakes.
I help others who are unable to help themselves.
I encourage others to be independent if they are capable of taking care of themselves.
I encourage others to grow and mature.
I resist helping those who can help themselves.
I support others' decisions to support themselves.
I avoid doing things people can do for themselves.
I show my love for others by allowing them to assume responsibility for their lives.

* * *

Afterword

Now that you've read *Maximum Self-Esteem*, please do one more thing: take a few minutes to imagine how joyful your life would be if you put the principles you've read about here into practice. It is true doing so involves a fair amount of effort. True also, that the process may not be speedy. But there is no question in my mind that the time and effort I spent were more than worth it; they earned me happiness and peace of mind I could achieve no other way. If I could take the feeling inside me today and share it with you, you would know at once what I mean. Since I can't, I hope this book has given you at least a glimpse of it.

I leave you with a final affirmation, one I encourage you to repeat every day:

**"I will do whatever I must
to improve my self-esteem."**

Appendix

SELF-ESTEEM INVENTORY TWO

Follow the same rating procedure you used for the first Inventory.

$1 = $ I NEVER do
$2 = $ I OCCASIONALLY do
$3 = $ I USUALLY do
$4 = $ I ALWAYS do

1) I maintain control of my emotions.
2) I do not blame my problems and mistakes on others.
3) I do not expect people to change just to please me.
4) I feel good no matter what circumstances come my way.
5) I willingly accept life as it is, no matter how I want it to be.
6) I am responsible for what goes on in my life.
7) I meet my own needs before I meet the needs of others.
8) I do not allow harmful habits to control my actions.
9) I do not try to trick people into doing as I wish.
10) I am not obligated to do things just because others ask me to.
11) My value as a human being is as great as anyone else's.
12) I avoid becoming involved in unnecessary details.
13) I do not judge my worth by comparing myself with anyone else.
14) My accomplishments have no bearing on my worth as a person.
15) Others' opinions of me are less important than my own.
16) I accept the consequences of my actions, but I do not feel guilty because of them.
17) I forgive myself when I make mistakes.
18) I do not try to impress others.
19) I do not dwell on unpleasant memories.
20) I accept people without judging them or their behavior.

21) I am as valuable and worthwhile as anyone in the world.
22) I do not accept responsibility for causing anyone else's emotions.
23) I give myself the same honor and respect I give others.
24) I keep an open mind on all subjects.
25) I do not protect others from the consequences of their actions.

Add all the numbers to arrive at the percentile. Listed below are the numbers of the statements, followed by the number of the chapter to which they relate.

1 - Chapter 7	14 - Chapter 5
2 - Chapter 19	15 - Chapter 11
3 - Chapter 6	16 - Chapter 10
4 - Chapter 18	17 - Chapter 9
5 - Chapter 17	18 - Chapter 11
6 - Chapter 19	19 - Chapter 8
7 - Chapter 22	20 - Chapter 6
8 - Chapter 16	21 - Chapter 5
9 - Chapters 14, 15	22 - Chapter 7
10 - Chapters 14, 15	23 - Chapter 20
11 - Chapter 5	24 - Chapter 21
12 - Chapters 13	25 - Chapter 22
13 - Chapter 12	

Repeat this inventory at intervals to review your progress, then set new goals for yourself. Remember, the purpose of this inventory is to provide you with feedback. Do not blame, criticize, or judge yourself negatively as a result of it. Instead, put your energy into additional determination.

*

Chapter References

(Chapter references also listed in the Bibliography are listed here by only title and author. Please check Bibliography for the complete information.)

Preface

1. *Reason and Emotion in Psychotherapy*, by Dr. Albert Ellis.
2. *Toward a Psychology of Being*, Second Edition, by Abraham Maslow.

Chapter 3 WHY WE HAVE POOR SELF-ESTEEM

J. Krishnamurti, *Think on These Things*, copyright 1964 by Krishnamurti Writings, Inc. New York: Perennial Library, Harper & Row, Publishers, Inc.

Chapter 4 MAKING CHANGES

Tarthang Tulku, *Skillful Means*.

Chapter 5 ACCEPTING OURSELVES

Benjamin Hoff, *The Tao of Pooh*, copyright 1982 by Benjamin Hoff. New York: Penguin Books.

Chapter 6 NEEDING APPROVAL

Marcus Aurielius, *Meditations*, Book IV.

Chapter 7 EMOTIONAL PAIN

1. P.D. Ouspensky, *The Fourth Way*, copyright 1957 by Tatiana M. Nagro. New York: Vintage Books, Random House.
2. Charles T. Tart, *Waking Up: Overcoming the Obstacles to Human Potential*, copyright 1986 by the Institute of Noetic Sciences. Boston: Shambhala Publications, Inc.

Chapter 9 MAKING MISTAKES

Joseph Conrad, *Outcast of the Islands*.

Chapter 10 GUILT

Reprinted from *Handbook to Higher Consciousness*, by Ken Keyes, Jr., Fifth Edition, Copyright 1975 by the Living Love Center.

Chapter 11 CHANGING OTHERS

1. Mark Twain, *Pudd'nhead Wilson*.
2. Lewis F. Presnall, *Search for Serenity*, copyright 1958. Salt Lake City, UT: Utah Alcoholism Foundation.

Chapter 12 COMPETITION

1., 2. Alfie Kohn, *No Contest: The Case Against Competition*.

Chapter 13 PERFECTIONISM

1. Ralph Waldo Emerson, "Representative Men."
2. Dr. Gerald Kranzler, *You Can Change How You Feel: a Rational-Emotive Approach*.

Chapter 14 MANIPULATION

Tarthang Tulku, *Skillful Means*.

Chapter 16 HABITS

Ellen J. Langer, *Mindfulness*.

Chapter 17 UNREALISTIC EXPECTATIONS

1. Charles T. Tart, *Waking Up: Overcoming the Obstacles to Human Potential*, copyright 1986 by the Institute of Noetic Sciences. Boston: Shambhala Publications, Inc.
2. Andrew Weil, *The Natural Mind*, Revised Edition, copyright 1972, 1986 by Andrew Weil. Boston: Houghton Mifflin Company

Chapter 18 NEGATIVITY

1. *The Holy Bible*.
2. Epictetus, *The Enchiridion*.
3. Willard and Marguerite Beecher, *Beyond Success and Failure: Ways to Self-Reliance and Maturity*, copyright © 1966 by Willard and Marguerite Beecher. 1971. New York: Pocket Books.
4. Nisargadatta Maharaj, *I Am That*, copyright 1973 by Nisargadatta Maharaj. Durham, NC: The Acorn Press

Chapter 19 SOLVING PROBLEMS

Russell L. Ackoff, *The Art of Problem Solving*, copyright 1978 by John Wiley & Sons. New York: John Wiley & Sons, Inc.

Chapter 21 RELIGIOUS BELIEFS

1. Alan Watts, *The Book on the Taboo Against Knowing Who You Are,* copyright 1966 by Alan Watts. New York: Collier Books/The Macmillan Company.

2. Everett L. Shostrom, *Man, the Manipulator: The Inner Journey From Manipulation to Actualization*, copyright 1967 by Abingdon Press. Nashville, TN: Abingdon Press.

3. Thomas Paine, *The Age of Reason.*

4. Ralph Waldo Emerson, "Self-Reliance."

Chapter 22 HELPING OTHERS

Nisargadatta Maharaj, *I Am That*, copyright 1973 by Nisargadatta Maharaj. Durham, NC: The Acorn Press.

*

Bibliography
and
Recommended Reading List

Anthony, Dr. Robert, *The Ultimate Secrets of Total Self-Confidence*, New York: Berkley Books, 1979.

Barksdale, L. S., *Essays on Self-Esteem*, Idyllwild, CA: The Barksdale Foundation, 1977.

Beck, Charlotte Joko, *Everyday Zen: Love & Work*, San Francisco: Harper & Row, 1989.

Beck, Deva, R.N., and James Beck, R.N., *The Pleasure Connection: How Endorphins Affect Our Health and Happiness*, San Marcos, CA: Synthesis Press, 1987.

Beecher, Willard and Marguerite, *Beyond Success and Failure: Ways to Self-Reliance and Maturity*, New York: Pocket Books, 1971.

Benson, Herbert, M.D., *Your Maximum Mind*, New York: Random House, Inc., 1987.

Branden, Nathaniel, *How to Raise Your Self-Esteem*, New York: Bantam Books, 1987.

Briggs, Dorothy, *Celebrate Your Self*, Garden City, NY: Doubleday and Company, 1977.

Burns, David D., M.D., *Feeling Good: The New Mood Therapy*, New York: New American Library, 1980.

Dyer, Dr. Wayne W., *Your Erroneous Zones*, New York: Avon Books, 1977. *Pulling Your Own Strings*, New York: Avon Books, 1979. *The Sky's the Limit*, New York: Pocket Books, 1981.

Ellis, Dr. Albert, *Reason and Emotion in Psychotherapy*, Secaucus, NJ: The Citadel Press, 1962.

Gawain, Shakti, *Creative Visualization*, New York: Bantam Books, 1978.

Justice, Blair, Ph.D., *Who Gets Sick*, Los Angeles: Jeremy P. Tarcher, Inc., 1988.

Kohn, Alfie, *No Contest: The Case Against Competition*, Boston: Houghton Mifflin Company, 1986.

Kranzler, Gerald, *You Can Change How You Feel: A Rational-Emotive Approach*, Eugene, OR: RETC Press. 1974

Langer, Ellen J., *Mindfulness*, New York: Addison-Wesley Publishing Co., 1989.

Maslow, Abraham. *Toward a Psychology of Being*, New Jersey: Van Nostrand, Inc., 1962

Maultsby, Maxie, M.D., *Coping Better...Anytime, Anywhere*, New York: Prentice Hall Press, 1986.

McKay, Matthew, Ph.D., and Patrick Fanning, *Self-Esteem*, New York: St. Martin's Press, 1988.

Miller, Angelyn, *The Enabler: When Helping Harms the Ones You Love*, Claremont, CA: Hunter House, 1988.

Missildine, W. Hugh, *Your Inner Child of the Past*, New York: Pocket Books, 1963.

Paine, Thomas, *The Age of Reason*, Baltimore, MD: Ottenheimer.

Schuller, Robert H., *Self-Esteem: The New Reformation*, Waco, TX: Word Books, 1982.

Seligman, Martin E. P., Ph.D., *Learned Optimism*, New York: Borzoi Books, Alfred A. Knopf, Inc., 1991

Smith, Manuel J., *When I Say No I Feel Guilty*, New York: Bantam Books, 1975.

Tulku, Tarthang, *Skillful Means: Gentle Ways to Successful Work*, Berkeley, CA: Dharma Publishing, 1978.

Copyright Acknowledgements

About the Author

Perpetually curious, author JERRY MINCHINTON has read extensively about self-esteem, as well as Eastern philosophies and religions. He combines the insight he's gained from these studies with practical business experience to shed light on some age-old problems of human behavior.

Jerry earned a B.A. with Highest Honors and a Master of Arts degree in Music at Eastern Washington University. He continued his education with doctoral studies at Florida State University.

An accomplished musician, he performed professionally for a number of years before founding a mail processing company. After guiding the firm through twelve years of steady growth, he withdrew from his CEO position to devote more time to the study of self-esteem.

Until recently a long-time resident of the Pacific Northwest, Jerry now lives and works in the beautiful Ozark Mountains of Southern Missouri, where he continues to indulge his obsession with self-esteem. He is a member of the National Council for Self Esteem and American MENSA.